QUILTING

with

LIBERTY.
FABRICS

QUILTING

with

LIBERTY.
FABRICS

---

15 Quilts Celebrating
145 Years in Fabric

JENNI SMITH

Published in 2020 by Lucky Spool Media, LLC
www.luckyspool.com
info@luckyspool.com

Text © Jenni Smith
Editor Susanne Woods
Designer Rae Ann Spitzenberger
Illustrations Kari Vojtechovsky

Photographs pages 1, 4, 9, 13, 16, 19–23, 39, 51, 60, 61, 65,
73, 85, 95, 103, 111, 119, 126, 131, 139, 149, 157, 165, 173,
176–186 © Liberty Fabric Limited

Photograph page 106 by Christopher White

All other photography © Page + Pixel, LLC

9 8 7 6 5 4 3 2 1

First Edition
Printed in China

Library of Congress Cataloging-in-Publication
Data available upon request

ISBN 978-1-940655-46-8

LSID0056

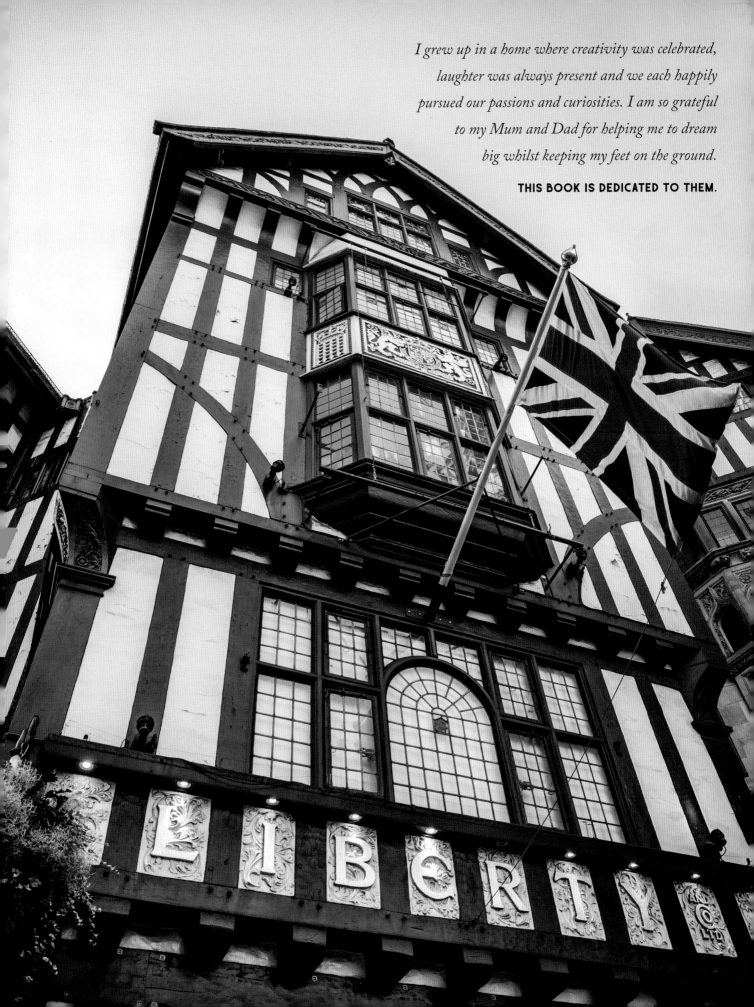

I grew up in a home where creativity was celebrated, laughter was always present and we each happily pursued our passions and curiosities. I am so grateful to my Mum and Dad for helping me to dream big whilst keeping my feet on the ground.

THIS BOOK IS DEDICATED TO THEM.

CONTENTS

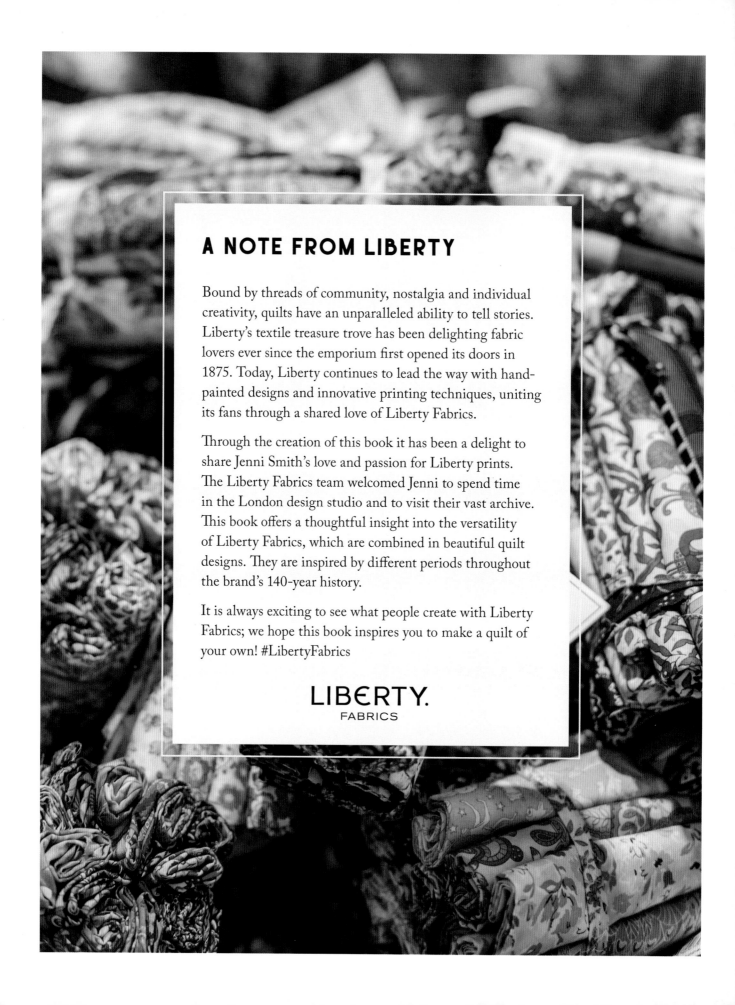

A NOTE FROM LIBERTY

Bound by threads of community, nostalgia and individual creativity, quilts have an unparalleled ability to tell stories. Liberty's textile treasure trove has been delighting fabric lovers ever since the emporium first opened its doors in 1875. Today, Liberty continues to lead the way with hand-painted designs and innovative printing techniques, uniting its fans through a shared love of Liberty Fabrics.

Through the creation of this book it has been a delight to share Jenni Smith's love and passion for Liberty prints. The Liberty Fabrics team welcomed Jenni to spend time in the London design studio and to visit their vast archive. This book offers a thoughtful insight into the versatility of Liberty Fabrics, which are combined in beautiful quilt designs. They are inspired by different periods throughout the brand's 140-year history.

It is always exciting to see what people create with Liberty Fabrics; we hope this book inspires you to make a quilt of your own! #LibertyFabrics

LIBERTY.
FABRICS

FOREWORD

Nobody has a casual fling with Liberty Fabrics. It is a true
romance. We speak of iconic prints as if they are cherished
friends. The beauty of each individual design brings us joy.
The charming, unique motifs — brimming with history,
keep on drawing us back for more.

When I begin sewing with my stash of Liberty Fabrics
I am instantly happy. All of my senses come alive. The
cottons feel heavenly and are literally a feast for the eyes.
Familiar prints that have been a constant for many years
make me feel comfortable. They evoke happy memories.
My mind is always curious to know the stories in these
surface patterns and I simply never tire of creating with
them. I collect new delights each season, share small pieces
with my friends and love observing the magic of what
inspiring people make with them around the world.

The specialness of Liberty Fabrics makes it hard to commit
to cut into them. Yet, for me that is the most exciting
part. A quilt stitched from prints you love dearly, is a quilt
that deserves to be made. True romance sometimes
requires sacrifice!

This book is a celebration of my passion for Liberty Fabrics.
Thank you for joining me on this creative adventure.

MY LIBERTY

I was born to be a collector of fabric. Childhood memories for me frequently involve a favourite item of clothing, the soft touch of an outfit pulled from our enormous dressing-up box, the textures and patterns of the upholstery in our home. I held on to remnants from my favourite dresses and duvets, never imagining a future purpose for them, but aware that I felt a special connection and would be sad to let them go.

I rarely visited London as a child, so early memories of Liberty prints are from the mill shop in Lancashire and also in the homes of my friends on cushions, curtains and Liberty beanie toy frogs. Oh how I wanted one of those!

At University I studied History of Art and developed a real passion for decoding the signs and symbols hidden in paintings. I was equally fascinated by the role of art movements in social history and the power of storytelling through visual mediums as well as the written word.

Not long after graduating, I spent a year living in Toronto where my quilting journey began. What started as a happy distraction when my first child napped, soon became a hugely important creative outlet for me. On my return to the UK, I began to share this craft with many others, through teaching. Gradually my hobby became a job that allowed me play with fabrics daily, sew beautiful handmade items to decorate my home, and to make connections with like-minded people.

Liberty Fabrics came back into my life with a bang with the birth of my daughter Edie. I made her a pair of bloomers in Tana Lawn™ in 2008 and, feeling grown up, I decided I could start a collection of my favourite prints to sew with. Many sweet outfits followed, and my interest in the heritage of the prints I was using, grew with several book publications about Liberty and an increasing awareness of exciting collaborations and seasonal collections the Design Studio produced. A few moments in particular stand out. In 2011 Liberty joined forces with musician Edwyn Collins and produced the print, Ornithology.

Facing page: Jenni with her Argyll Quilt in the Liberty Heritage Suite.

Edwyn suffered a double brain haemorrhage in 2005 and as part of his rehabilitation he began to draw sketches of different birds each day, dating them and visibly developing a beautiful line as the months passed by. I worked on an exhibition of these drawings with my friend Andy at the 108 Gallery in Harrogate and was so moved by the story, and meeting Edwyn and his brilliant wife Grace, that I bought his sketch of a puffin.

Can you imagine how excited I was to discover just months later that Edwyn's drawings were going to be on Tana Lawn, and that my puffin was included in the design?

The quilt I sleep beneath each night is made from this fabric, combined with more Liberty delights and remnants of my wedding dress appliquéd onto it. It's a quilt with a story based on resilience and love.

Jenni, wearing her precious Manning print, with her studio manager Kay Walsh.

Two years later, I remember desperately trying to get a mobile phone signal while on holiday in a rural Tuscan farmhouse. I wanted to order the new Manning iceberg print on Tana Lawn in the colourway I had set my heart on. We arrived home, having spent quite a lot of money. I deliberately opened the front door first so that I could swiftly grab the Liberty parcel and hide it in my sewing room to avoid having to explain why I couldn't live without it.

In 2015 I was accepted to share a textile picture I had stitched using Liberty, in a book published to celebrate the company's 140th birthday. I loved reading personal accounts of how Liberty had been part of other makers' lives over the years.

By 2016 I found myself a curious quilter, who loves Liberty, and history, and who was realising that you can use the medium of fabric and thread to tell personal, intriguing stories with soul. I am a born daydreamer and in the chaos of everyday life, the idea of writing this book began to grow. What if I could celebrate the incredible journey of Liberty, through 15 decades of outstanding fabric design, with a quilt project reflecting each step of the way? Surely that would add a whole new level of interest for makers and be a challenge to research. I could visit the archive and inspire Liberty fans to sew special heirlooms of their own with my unique designs. I swiftly concluded that I would try my hardest to find a way to make this happen.

One year later I was lucky to make connections with members of the Liberty design team while they developed their quilting collections. This gave me the opportunity to design projects that showcased the fabrics. Building that relationship was really important and enabled me to move forward with my dream.

Seeing this book become a reality, fills me with happiness and pride. Having an excuse to design and sew with Liberty fabrics on a daily basis for many months has been a real pleasure. Like most quilters, my next projects are just waiting to get onto the cutting table.

I hope you enjoy using this book as much as I have enjoyed writing it and thank you to Liberty for having such an incredible past to explore and to celebrate in my favourite creative medium.

LIBERTY

THEN
and
NOW

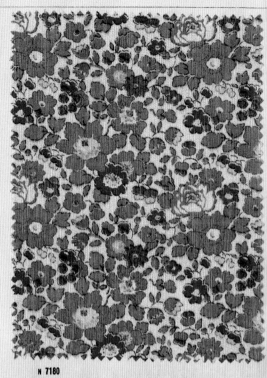

Length of Pieces: 40 yds.
Width: 38 ins.   Price
Guaranteed Fast Colours.

N 7180

LIBERTY & Cᵒ·, Lᵀᴰ·   LONDON.

THE ANATOMY OF A LIBERTY PRINT

When I embarked upon writing this book, I challenged myself to learn more about the anatomy of a Liberty print. There is no doubt that each one is extraordinary, but why is that exactly?

After spending time behind the scenes, observing different members of the Liberty team at work, and asking lots of questions, I discovered that the following five elements all contribute to the success of each fabric print: The Archive, The Design Studio, The Mechanics of Printing, The Base Cloth and The Haberdashery. All of these are impressive in their own right, and combined, they create a winning formula that is hard to rival. I'm happy to share my insights here.

THE ARCHIVE

History is a boundless source of inspiration and Liberty has an archive which contains approximately 50,000 prints. When I first read that figure I was pretty overwhelmed! It is extremely fortunate that these were looked after during the time Liberty owned the print works at Merton and they are now housed outside the city in a temperature-controlled building. There is also a small archive room in the London office, which I have been fortunate to visit.

Sample books, drawings, fabric remnants and physical objects such as carved wood blocks for printing, often provide the spark for contemporary fabric collections. On occasion the entire repeat of a pattern does not exist, but just a fragment can be the start of an exciting new design.

Anna Buruma is the in-house Head Archivist at Liberty and has worked with the company for over 20 years. She has an incredible knowledge, combined with genuine passion and she ensures that this unrivalled resource is used to its full potential. A highlight for me was showing Anna my Eclectic quilt made up from my personal collection of Liberty prints, and listening to her recount fascinating stories related to them.

The Liberty archive is a fine example of cherishing the past to create for the future.

Facing page, top right: This swatch shows an original colourway of the much loved Liberty Classic 'Betsy' from the 1930s.

THE DESIGN STUDIO

The Liberty Design Studio was born in 1952. Before that, fabric designs were commissioned from people working outside the company. Now it is home to fifteen artists who work in a space connected to Liberty's Tudor building by a wooden bridge. They design approximately 18 months in advance, so a lot of their work is top secret! I have only had a sneak peek of day-to-day life in the Studio, but it was very memorable.

Each person is a specialist in different techniques of hand drawing and painting, as well as having experience in the technical textile design skills required to create a Liberty Fabrics design.

I love that in a digital age most of the Liberty Fabrics designs start with painting and drawing. Within each collection, different media are celebrated from watercolour, oil, pen and ink to etching. They conceptualise, re-work and hand-draw prints that translate into seasonal fabrics and collections.

Each Liberty print is then given a name which I pride myself on trying to learn and which, in my opinion, adds personality and intrigue. It is never random — there is always a story to discover! Sometimes it could be after people — from royalty to artists as with Xanthe and Gustav & Otto,

The hand drawn motifs used to create the design Kew Trellis, were inspired by Art Nouveau botanicals from the Liberty archive.

or after a location visited as with Tresco, one of my all-time favourite floral prints.

I have been so lucky to have input from the Design Team for this book, especially when selecting the perfect fabrics for each of my quilt designs. I really admire their ability to push stylistic boundaries and be cutting-edge, whilst honouring the brand's heritage at the same time.

THE MECHANICS OF PRINT

First and foremost, Liberty Fabrics are print specialists and have been since the company began in 1875. They were block printing cottons before they designed exquisite patterns of their own and the exceptional print quality of every metre of fabric they produce, has earned their world-class reputation.

In the past 15 decades, print technology has evolved and Liberty has always been a forerunner in mastering new techniques. At present, they use the traditional method of screen printing as well as modern digital printing. I am always blown away by the colour saturation and the amazing level of detail that can be achieved in every inch of fabric.

Today they have their own mill in the North of Italy, close to Lake Como, where each year millions of metres of fabric are transformed from plain white cotton into dazzling designs. A trip to see this magical process in real life, is definitely on my wish-list.

Above: Carving a design into a wood block and printing using a wood block.

Facing page: Tresco is digitally printed at the Liberty Print works in Italy. Digital printing enables the designer to maintain the painted quality from the original artwork onto fabric.

Small test screens, as shown in this picture, are used to trial designs and colourways before committing to bulk print runs.

col 8

29

Different colours of inks ready to be trialed for a screen print. Every colour within a Liberty print is specially mixed to a unique dye recipe.

BASE CLOTH

Stroking Tana Lawn is a common pastime for Liberty fans worldwide and I often hear "how can it be cotton when it feels like silk?". As a child, my Nanny Gladys took me to the Liberty Mill shop and it is the feel of the fabric I remember the most. I knew I had to take some home with me, so at the tender age of eight, I started my Liberty collection.

Only a few years ago, I learned how the name Tana Lawn came about. The answer was from my elderly neighbour Brenda, who hung out her prized vintage Liberty shirts on the washing line each week — proof also of the fabric's durability.

Liberty's world-famous Tana Lawn fabric traces as far back as the 1910s. It was named after Lake Tana in East Africa, the place where the particular kind of cotton plant grew and from which came a fibre with a very long staple, producing a very fine thread. After the First World War, Liberty's fabric buyer William Haynes Dorell, greatly encouraged the production and printing of Tana Lawn. The combination of this luxuriously soft fabric together with predominantly small, delicate, floral prints was such a success, that it swiftly became Liberty's bestselling fabric. Lasenby Cotton was introduced to Liberty Fabrics in 2017 and is named after Liberty's founder Arthur Lasenby Liberty. The 100% cotton fabric has been especially designed for quilters. This new substrate is a little heavier than Tana Lawn which makes it perfect for craft projects and classic patchwork quilting.

This close-up shows the different weave of Lasenby Cotton (left) and Tana Lawn. Both achieve deep penetration of ink dyes and exquisite detail.

THE HABERDASHERY

Visiting the haberdashery on the third floor of Liberty is unforgettable and something that has delighted customers throughout each decade of its history. This unique creative space exudes style and artistic flair. Fabric lovers worldwide make pilgrimages to the haberdashery department, and are charmed by its history, character and the visual feast of endless bolts of Liberty prints laid out before them. I find it physically impossible to leave without a little piece of Liberty for a craft project, as does everyone I know who visits. Online fabric shopping is perfectly fine, but having a designated space to celebrate Liberty Fabrics, accentuates the experience. I always come away feeling energised and inspired whilst secretly planning when I can go back again!

Now that you know all about the fabrics in this book, let's discover the quilt patterns that you can follow to make beautiful heirlooms to treasure.

THE
SEWING
BOX

TOOLS

Whilst sewing in my own studio space and teaching many people to quilt over the years, I have tried and tested numerous tools and notions. It is important not to feel you can't begin a quilt without having the perfect equipment. People have made beautiful quilts without these for decades! However, I always find personal recommendations from fellow sewists reassuring and helpful. So, here are a few of my favourite things.

CUTTING MAT

Self-healing mats enable cutting through multiple layers of fabric. Choose a size which is workable in your sewing space. Remember, the bigger you can go the better. Folding mats are handy to store and take away on crafty weekends. A mat with degree markings is also very helpful.

ROTARY CUTTER

This is used together with your cutting mat. My favourite is an Olfa 45mm straight handle. There are many options available, so try them out when you can, to see which you find the most comfortable. I also use an 18mm blade for small curves and cutting around templates. You will need to change the blade when cutting becomes a trial — don't leave it too long, especially before cutting into your treasured Liberty stash!

QUILTING RULER

This is an essential tool for quiltmaking. Choose one which correlates with the size of your cutting mat, so if you have a large mat you might want to consider a 6" × 24" ruler. My main criterion when choosing rulers is clear visibility of the quarter inch markings. A 6½" square can prove very useful for

trimming down blocks and I wouldn't be without mine. The Add-a-Quarter Plus ruler is very useful when Foundation Paper Piecing. It helps to fold the paper and trim away the correct seam allowance.

SEWING MACHINE

The main considerations when sewing Liberty fabrics, are choosing the correct needle size and thread for each particular fabric (page 31) and ensuring your tension settings are correct. Tana Lawn is finely woven and if your sewing machine has the option of a straight stitch needle plate, this really makes a difference. It basically means that beneath the needle there is only a small hole through which the stitch is made, and less room for fine fabric such as Tana Lawn to be pushed underneath and caught. I sew on a Janome Memory Craft 9450 QCP but I have had lots of creative fun on their more basic models over the years.

THIMBLE

There are many options for protecting your fingertips when hand sewing. I am especially comfortable with a soft leather thimble which moulds to your finger shape with repeated use.

NEEDLES

Use the correct needles for your machine, as generic needles may not be the same quality. For Tana Lawn a fine needle is essential. I would recommend using a 70/10 when piecing. For Lasenby Cotton, an 80/12 needle is perfect. This size would also work well for quilting both fabrics.

For hand-sewing I vary the needles depending on the project, but I mainly switch between Tulip appliqué needles and John James sharps.

THREAD

In order to get the best results, it makes sense to match a cotton fabric with a cotton thread. When you are assembling blocks, seams lay flatter with a fine 50wt thread. Polyester is too harsh and if it needs to be unpicked it can damage your fabric. My preference is to use Aurifil and every quilt in this book has been sewn up with their amazing array of colours. I love the creative possibilities of using different thread weights and I would also recommend trying their 80wt which is the finest weight, for needle-turn appliqué and English Paper Piecing. The stitches will melt into your project and become barely visible. The heavier 12wt is ideal for hand quilting or for a bolder machine quilting stitch.

PINS AND PINCUSHIONS

Fine sharp pins are really important if you don't want to snag your fabric. Tulip patchwork pins are a great all-rounder. Tulip appliqué pins are shorter in length and ideal for use in needle-turn appliqué when sewing on small shapes. I love collecting

pincushions and my Frida Kahlo and David Hockney ones (page 29) are by Yorkshire Ceramicist Katch Skinner. Hanging out with these two creative icons makes me happy!

WASHI TAPE

I love how pretty washi tape looks in my studio, but I also use it frequently on my sewing machine to create a visual guide when stitching snowball corners or different seam allowances. It doesn't leave a sticky residue after use and can be re-positioned easily.

SCISSORS

I choose scissors that feel comfortable in my hand and that are sharp enough that they snip right to the tips of the blades. For large cuts of fabric, I use my Ernest Wright 8.25" Dressmaker Shears and for trimming threads and appliqué I use their Antique Storks. Reserve a pair of craft scissors for paper. Don't ever be tempted to use fabric scissors as it will dull the blades.

SEAM RIPPER

Sewing machines may come with a free seam ripper though I prefer one with an ergonomic handle, especially if it is going to get plenty of use.

STILETTO

This looks like a long needle, but is more robust. It will reach beneath the presser foot of your sewing machine to hold the fabric in position, where your fingers cannot reach. It sounds like a luxury but the more it is used, the more of a necessity it becomes.

HERA MARKER

An inexpensive plastic tool used for scoring temporary lines onto a quilt top before stitching.

QUILTING CLIPS

These clips are useful on bulky projects and when sewing down the binding on a quilt.

DAYLIGHT LAMP

This is a recent addition to my sewing studio and now I can't imagine how I ever managed without one. I have a floor lamp which I set up next to my sewing machine or move to a cosy chair when I'm hand sewing.

PRESSING MAT

A wool pressing mat can be used on any flat surface. It prevents your patchwork slipping, and transfers the heat from your iron to the underside of your fabric, as well as to the top. For piecing projects it is really useful, though it doesn't offer the same surface area as an ironing board.

GLUE PEN

These are so useful when Foundation Paper Piecing and can also be used instead of basting thread in English Paper Piecing. My favourite is the Prym Aqua Glue Marker which is yellow when applied, but then disappears when washed.

BASTING

I always keep a can of Odif 505 basting spray in my studio which makes joining the layers of a quilt sandwich easy. For hand basting I use a cotton basting thread, so I don't harm the fibres of the quilt when I remove the temporary stitches.

TABLE BRUSH SET

In a bid to keep my workspace tidy, especially after Foundation Paper Piecing, I use a beautiful, handmade brush set by Iris Hantverk. It is brilliant for sweeping up threads too.

MARKING PENCILS

A pencil with a retractable lead ensures a consistently fine line, which is important for accuracy. I like the Sewline Pencil Trio with 3 lead colours.

THREAD GLOSS

Sew Fine Thread Gloss is applied to your sewing thread before hand-stitching. It avoids tangles and smells nice too!

POINT TURNER

Poking scissors into the corners of a project will never end well, so buying a point turner is a much better option. I especially like my bamboo one, rather than plastic.

TECHNIQUES

The quilts in this book have been designed to use an exciting variety of techniques including appliqué, English Paper Piecing (EPP), Foundation Paper Piecing (FPP) and sewing curves. For an overview of these techniques see Quilting Basics (page 187). If you are entirely new to quilt making, welcome! There is a free downloadable PDF of Quiltmaking Basics on the Lucky Spool website to help get you started on your journey. It contains a lot of the quilting terms, tools and methods for creating beautiful quilts, so please do use that as an extensive resource and let me know how you get on.

Most quilts are designed to be made using a sewing machine, but hand piecing is an option and projects such as Meadow and Bishopsgate are hand sewn and portable.

TEMPLATES

Templates for individual quilts can be found on pages 194–221. Do ensure that all templates have been copied to the correct size before cutting into your fabric.

FABRIC ALLOWANCE

The two main Liberty Fabrics used in the projects are Tana Lawn and Lasenby Cotton. Tana Lawn is lighter in weight than the Lasenby Cotton, but it is perfectly fine to combine the two as in Argyll, Blossom, Love and Kisses, and Oscar.

Please note that Tana Lawn has a usable width of 52" and Lasenby Cotton has a usable width of 42". The materials for each quilt are listed according to the exact fabrics used, so if you do make changes, don't forget to adjust the quantities you need to buy. If you are using a quilting cotton in place of a Tana Lawn, add an additional 25-30% to the suggested yardage.

THINK LIKE ARTHUR LIBERTY

Channel the brave and curious spirit of Liberty's founder and have a go at quilt projects that you may feel are out of your comfort zone. Start with a simply pieced project and try the more challenging quilts as you gain confidence.

SHARE YOUR QUILTS

I am truly excited to see what you make using the patterns from this book. Please share them on social media using #quiltingwithliberty, #libertycraftclub and tag me @jennismithsews.

LIBERTY FABRICS REFERENCING

For ease of reference in each project, I have given each fabric a colour. This is simply by way of a visual and organisational aid. There are a few fabrics where a single colour reference was not possible. I do stress it is not official Liberty terminology to use colour labelling. Please refer to The Swatches (page 176–186) for the official Liberty nomenclature for each fabric. This is the name followed by a letter, or a unique code ending in the same letter.

THE PROJECTS

ARTHUR

One of Liberty's best-loved prints, Hera, is largely credited to Arthur Silver, the founder of the Silver Studio. Designed in 1887 and first printed by Liberty furnishing fabrics in the mid 1890s, Hera quickly became intrinsically linked to Liberty and remains an iconic symbol of the company's heritage. The peacock feather was a fashionable and much used symbol during the Aesthetic movement of the 1880s.

I designed the blocks in the Arthur Quilt to give the impression of peacock feathers and to reflect this flamboyant period. They are made from half square triangles and stripped piecing, joined on the bias. The square layout mirrors a coveted Liberty Hera scarf, and these provide great ideas for the endless colour combinations you could use for this project.

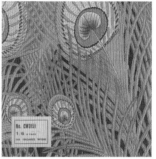

I was drawn to the Liberty Hesketh House quilting collection because it features a new design named Pipers Peacock which, along with prints from the Summer House Quilting Collection, I couldn't resist. I would recommend a pop of colour for the centre of the feather eye and for the central unit of the quilt.

This quilt celebrates Sir Arthur Lasenby Liberty, who founded Liberty back in 1875. Arthur was the son of a draper with an eye for exquisite detail, a sharp business sense and plenty of entrepreneurial spirit. He valued skilled craftsmanship immensely and his first venture with fabrics as an independent retailer, was to develop new dyes for the silks he imported. These became instantly desirable and were known as Liberty Art Colours. Next, Arthur wanted to sell printed fabrics and so he began to commission surface patterns, the first ones being inspired by Indian woodblock designs. Demand from the public was high, and exciting collaborations with companies such as the Silver Studio began.

I am sure that your version will demand attention, just as a peacock does!

From top: Sir Arthur Lasenby Liberty, Archive Hera, Pipers Peacock, Nouveau Mayflower.

ARTHUR

Finished Quilt Size: 88" square • *Finished Block Size:* 8"

MATERIALS

Pipers Peacock Orange:
2½ yards (2.29 m)

Cumbrian Vine Grey:
4¼ yards (3.89 m)

Chiltern Hill Pink:
⅝ yard (57 cm)

Wiltshire Shade Blue:
⅜ yard (34 cm)

Cumbrian Vine Orange:
⅜ yard (34 cm)

Victoria Floral Red:
¼ yard (23 cm)

Pipers Peacock Blue:
1¾ yards (1.6 m)

Nouveau Mayflower Blue:
1½ yards (1.37 m) (or 2½
yards (2.29 m) if you want
the border print to be
directional)

*Wiltshire Shade Blue for
the binding:*
¾ yard (69 cm)

*Harriet's Pansy Blue for
the backing:*
8 yards (7.32 m)

Batting: 96" × 96"
(2.44 m × 2.44 m)

Fine chalk pencil

Cutting mat with 45-degree
angle marking

CUTTING

*From the Pipers Peacock
Orange, cut:*
(12) 4" × 42" strips,
subcut into:
   (112) 4" squares

(7) 1¾" × 42" strips,
subcut into:
   (20) 14" × 1¾" rectangles

(15) 1½" × 42" strips

*From the Cumbrian Vine
Grey, cut:*
(4) 10" × 42" strips,
subcut into:
   (13) 10" squares
   (2) 5½" squares

(6) 4½" × 42" strips,
subcut into:
   (48) 4½" squares

(7) 2½" × 42" strips,
subcut into:
   (112) 2½" squares

(20) 2" × 42" strips

(10) 1½" × 42" strips

*From the Chiltern Hill
Pink, cut:*
(7) 2½" × 42" strips,
subcut into:
   (112) 2½" squares

*From the Wiltshire Shade
Blue, cut:*
(9) 2½" × 42" strips for
the binding

(4) 2" × 42" strips

*From the Cumbrian Vine
Orange, cut:*
(4) 2½" × 42" strips

*From the Victoria Floral
Red, cut:*
(1) 5½" × 42" strip,
subcut into:
   (2) 5½" squares

(1) 1½" × 42" strip,
subcut into:
   (28) 1½" squares

*From the Pipers Peacock
Blue, cut:*
(3) 10" × 42" strips,
subcut into:
   (12) 10" squares

(6) 4½" × 42" strips,
subcut into:
   (48) 4½" squares

*From the Nouveau
Mayflower Blue, cut:*
(1) 10"× 42" strip, subcut into:
   (1) 10" square
   (4) 4½" squares

(9) 4½" × 42" strips

ASSEMBLING THE FEATHER BLOCK

1 Pin and sew together a 2" strip of Cumbrian Vine Grey with a 1½" strip of Pipers Peacock Orange, right sides together (RST). Press the seams in one direction on the wrong side, then turn and press from the right side to ensure the strips lay flat.

2 Referencing Figure 1, join a 1½" strip of Cumbria Vine Grey and a 1½" strip of Pipers Peacock Orange to the unit created in Step 1, alternating the two fabrics.

3 Repeat Step 2.

4 Finally, attach a 2" strip of Cumbrian Vine Grey at the bottom to complete the strip unit.

> TIP: *When sewing long strips together, pin carefully being sure the short ends are aligned. Alternating at which short end you begin stitching will prevent the strips from twisting out of shape as they are joined.*

5 Repeat Steps 1–4 to make a total of five strip units. Subcut each strip set into (4) 8½" units, making a total of 20 subcut units.

Figure 1

6 Using the 45-degree line on your cutting mat together with your ruler, cut 10 of the subcut units from Step 5 on a 45-degree angle from top left to bottom right. (Fig. 2)

Figure 2

7 Cut the remaining 10 units on a 45-degree angle from top right to bottom left (Fig. 3). Keep the resulting triangles in four separate piles: labelling them A, B, C and D.

Figure 3

8 Beginning with the A triangles, gently align the long edge of the triangle with a 14" × 1¾" Pipers Peacock Orange Unit E rectangle. Pin and sew the two together, pressing the seam towards the rectangle.

9 To ensure proper alignment of the feather, position the assembled unit from Step 8 with the wrong side facing up. Aligning the ruler marking with the raw edge of the rectangle, and the edge of the ruler with the triangle seam intersection of the first barb of the strip set A triangle, draw a line at a right angle across the width of the rectangle (Fig. 4). Continue to do this from every point where a barb connects to the rectangle, for a total of six markings. Finally, mark a vertical line ¼" away from the long raw edge of the rectangle. The points where these marks intersect are the alignment points for the barb seams when attaching the C triangle to the opposite side of the Unit E rectangle.

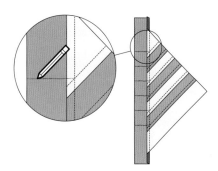

Figure 4

10 Position a strip set C triangle from Step 7 wrong side up. Mark a line parallel to the long edge of the Unit E rectangle ¼" away, to indicate the seam allowance.

11 With the C triangle and the assembled unit from Step 9 right sides facing, place a pin at each corresponding intersection of the barbs with the pins parallel to the short edge of the Unit E rectangle and sew (Fig. 5). Press Unit E seams towards the C triangle.

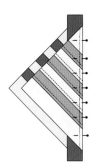

Figure 5

TIP: *Taking time to mark and pin these barb intersections may seem tedious, but doing so will maintain impressive accuracy when constructing this block.*

12 Press the block well. With the right side facing up, position a ruler ensuring that the smallest barb strips sit 2¼" away from the upper right corner and that the corner of the ruler is equidistant on the centre strip. Trim away excess, then turn the block and trim it to 8½" square. (Fig. 6)

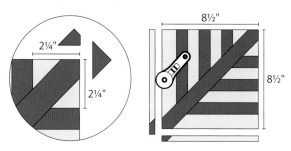

Figure 6

13 Repeat to create a total of 10 A/C left-leaning and 10 B/D right-leaning blocks.

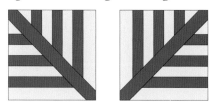

Make 10 of Each Block

ASSEMBLING THE EYE BLOCK

1 With the right sides together, position a 2½" Cumbrian Vine Grey square onto the top left corner of a 4" Pipers Peacock Orange square and a 2½" Chiltern Hill Pink square in the lower right corner, with the right sides together (RST). Referencing Figure 7 for placement and using a chalk pencil, draw a diagonal line on the wrong side of the squares and sew along the drawn line. Trim away the outer corner ¼" away from the sewn line and press towards the squares.

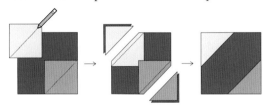

Figure 7

2 Repeat Step 1 to make 112 units and set them aside for now.

3 With the right sides together, pin and sew a 2" strip of Wiltshire Shade Blue to a 2½" Strip of Cumbrian Vine Orange. Press the seam towards the Blue fabric. Repeat to make four strip sets.

4 Subcut each assembled strip set from Step 3 into (28) 1½" × 4" rectangles for a total of 112 units. (Fig. 8)

Figure 8

5 Referencing Figure 9 for placement, attach a unit from Step 2 on either side of the unit from Step 4 and press towards the unit from Step 4. Repeat to make 56 units.

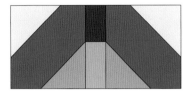

Figure 9

6 Referencing Figure 10 for placement, use the remaining units from Step 4 to attach to either side of a 1½" Victoria Floral Red square. Press the Red fabric outwards. Repeat to make 28 units.

Figure 10

7 Join together an assembled unit from Step 5 to either side of an assembled unit from Step 6, aligning the long edges and ensuring the seam intersections meet. Press. This block will measure 8½" square.

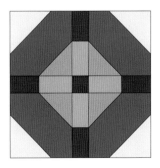

Make 28 Blocks

THE ARROW BLOCK
MAKING THE HALF-SQUARE TRIANGLES (HST)

1 Align the raw edges of one Cumbrian Vine Grey and one Pipers Peacock Blue 10" square with the right sides together. Using a chalk pencil, draw two diagonal lines on the wrong side of one square, creating an X.

2 Sew a ¼" seam on either side of the drawn lines from Step 1, creating 4 seams. Cut the square at the vertical midpoint and then again at the horizontal midpoint. Then cut each section along the drawn lines from Step 1, resulting in eight HST units. Press towards the Blue fabric and trim away the dog ears. (Fig. 11)

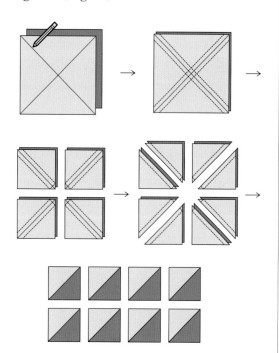

Figure 11

3 Repeat Step 1 with the remaining eleven pairs of 10" squares to make a total of 96 HST units.

ASSEMBLING THE ARROW BLOCK 4-PATCH

1 Referencing Figure 12 for placement, arrange two HST units with a 4½" Pipers Peacock Blue and Cumbrian Vine Grey square. Sew the two rows together along the short side and press the seams in opposite directions. Sew the assembled rows together on the long side, nesting the seams. Repeat to make a total of 48 Arrow Blocks, each measuring 8½" square.

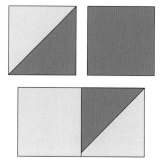

Figure 12

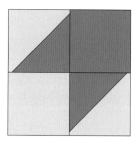

Make 48 Blocks

2 Do not press the final seam until you piece together the rows later.

CENTRE MEDALLION BLOCK

1 With the right sides together, position a 10" Cumbrian Vine Grey and Nouveau Mayflower Blue square. Repeat Steps 1 and 2 in Making the Half-Square Triangles (see facing page) to create a total of 8 HSTs.

2 Align the raw edges of a 5½" Cumbrian Vine Grey and a Victoria Floral Red square, right sides together. Draw a diagonal line on the wrong side of one square and sew a ¼" seam either side of the line. Cut along the drawn line and press. Trim the HSTs to 4½" square (Fig. 13). Repeat to make a total of 4 HSTs.

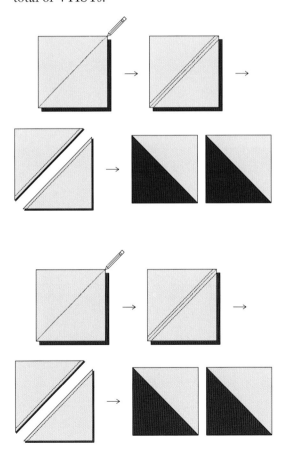

Figure 13

3 Using the HSTs and a 4½" Nouveau Mayflower Blue square, follow the instruction to create a 4-Patch (Fig. 12) opposite. Repeat to make (4) 4-Patch blocks, each measuring 8½" square. (Fig. 14)

Figure 14

Make 4 Blocks

ASSEMBLING THE QUILT TOP

1 Referencing Figure 15, arrange 12 Arrow Blocks, 7 Eye Blocks, 5 Feather Blocks and a Centre Medallion Block into a 5 × 5 grid. Piece the rows into a quadrant. Sew the blocks into five rows as shown. Press the seams of the Arrow blocks in opposite directions to nest the seams. For example: Row 1, block 1 press down, block 2 press up, block 3 press down, block 4 press up, block 5 press down.

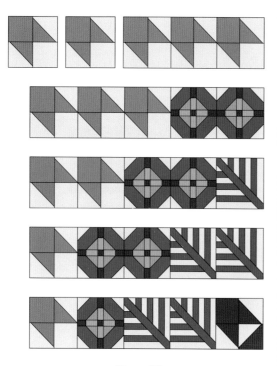

Figure 15

2 Repeat Step 1 to make a total of four quadrants, referencing the Assembly Diagram for block orientation.

3 Attach the four quadrants, referencing the Assembly Diagram (page 47) for placement.

4 Join (2) 4½" Nouveau Mayflower Blue strips together with a diagonal seam and trim to 80½". Repeat to make another 80½" Border strip.

5 Cut one 4½" Nouveau Mayflower Blue strip in half. Join one of these half-strips to two full 4½" strips with a diagonal seam. Trim to 88½". Repeat to make another 88½" Border strip.

6 Join the shorter borders to the left and right of the assembled unit from Step 3 and press outwards. Then join the longer borders to the top and bottom. Press the seams towards the borders.

BACKING

Cut the Harriet's Pansy Blue into 3 strips, each 96" long and join them together on their short side. This will allow an overhang around the quilt top to accommodate any movement when quilting.

QUILTING

The Arthur quilt has been long arm quilted with feathers and peacock inspired details, but a grid of straight lines would work equally well, because the design is so strong.

Assembly Diagram

STILE

From 1890, Liberty was very closely associated with the Art Nouveau style of decoration, so much so that this led to the Italians using the phrase "Stile Liberty" as a direct translation. Sinuous lines, inspired by natural forms and delicate florals were transferred onto fabric for artistic Liberty shoppers, as well as furniture and jewellery. One classic print from this time is Ianthe (1900) — still fascinating makers 120 years later.

Scottish architect and designer Charles Rennie Mackintosh was a key figure in the Art Nouveau movement, skillfully combining graphic elements with simplified curves. His legacy inspired the Liberty print Rennie and in turn, the design of this quilt. In fact, the quilting motif is a Charles Rennie Mackintosh rose which I was very excited to discover and which completes this quilt's story beautifully.

The fabric used is Summer House, printed on Lasenby Cotton. The Liberty Design Studio spent time drawing at the orangery in Kew Gardens to conceptualize this collection, observing details such as the wrought iron railings and trellis work. I totally fell in love with the Conservatory Fruits lemon design and this sparked the color scheme for the Stile quilt. Using this fabric for a border allows it to be seen in all its glory.

The large flower blocks are perfect for showcasing your favourite Liberty prints and you can add a lot of interest with the appliqué circles and borders. It is important to use the same fabric for the stripes as in the corners of your snowballs and sashing fabric. Doing this makes the flower blocks with the orange centres appear to be different from those blocks with the yellow centres. In fact, the top and bottom rows of the strip blocks are providing this additional framing, which makes the quilt top look more complex to piece than it actually is.

From top: Ianthe, Rennie, Kew Trellis

STILE

Finished Quilt Size: 61" × 75" • *Finished Block Size:* 7"

MATERIALS

Oxford Fern Cream:
2½ yards (2.29 m)

Cambridge Fern Blue:
1 yard (91 cm)

Victoria Floral Blue:
¾ yard (69 cm)

Kew Trellis Blue:
½ yard (46 cm)

Manor Tile Blue:
⅝ yard (57 cm)

Conservatory Fruits Yellow:
1 yard (91 cm)

Kona Kumquat Orange:
¾ yard (69 cm) including
the binding

Kona Citrus Yellow: fat eighth
(23 cm × 56 cm)

Hidcote Berry Blue: 4 yards
(3.66 m) for the backing

Batting: 69" × 83"
(1.75 m × 2.11 m)

Double-sided fusible web

Chalk pencil

Templates (see page 211)

CUTTING

From the Oxford Fern Cream, cut:

(25) 1½" × 42" strips, subcut one strip into:

(4) 1½" × 7½" rectangles

Reserve remaining
(24) 1½" × 42" strips

(3) 3½" × 42" strips, subcut into:

(64) 3½" × 1½" rectangles

(40) 1½" squares

(2) 7½" × 42" strips, subcut into:

(32) 7½" × 1½" rectangles

(120) 1½" squares

(11) 1½" × 42" strips, subcut four strips into:

(96) 1½" squares

Reserve remaining
(7) 1½" x 42" strips

From the Cambridge Fern Blue, cut:

(19) 1½" × 42" strips, subcut one strip into:

(3) 1½" × 7½" rectangles

Reserve remaining
(18) 1½" × 42" strips

From the Victoria Floral Blue, cut:

(7) 3½" × 42" strips, subcut into:

(80) 3½" squares

From the Kew Trellis Blue, cut:

(4) 3½" × 42" strips, subcut into:

(48) 3½" squares

From the Manor Tile Blue, cut: (7) 2½" × 42" strips

From the Conservatory Fruits Yellow, cut:
(8) 3½" × 42" strips

From the Kona Kumquat Orange, cut:
(7) 2½" × 42" binding strips

ASSEMBLING THE STRIPE BLOCK

1 Pin and sew together a 1½" × WOF strip of Oxford Fern Cream with a 1½" × WOF strip of Cambridge Fern Blue. Press the seam towards the Cambridge Fern Blue.

TIP: *When using strip sets, I recommend pressing first on the wrong side, then turning the unit over and pressing from the right side.*

2 Referencing Figure 1, join a second 1½" × WOF strip of Oxford Fern Cream and a second 1½" × WOF strip of Cambridge Fern Blue.

3 Repeat Step 2 with another 1½" × WOF strip of Oxford Fern Cream and 1½" × WOF strip of Cambridge Fern Blue, alternating the two fabrics.

4 Finally, attach a 1½" × WOF strip of Oxford Fern Cream at the bottom to complete the strip unit, pressing all seams toward the Cambridge Fern Blue. (Fig. 1)

Figure 1

5 Repeat Steps 1–4 to make a total of six strip units.

6 Subcut each strip unit into (5) 7½" square blocks, making a total of 30.

7 Because this quilt requires 31 Stripe Blocks, we are going to use the 1½" × 7½" fabric strips in the same colour order to create one more. Alternate the placement of the cream and blue strips to create the final 7½" square Stripe Block.

ASSEMBLING THE PARTIAL SNOWBALL BLOCKS

1 Using a chalk pencil, draw a diagonal line on the wrong side of the (256) 1½" Oxford Fern Cream squares.

2 With the right sides together, reference Figure 2 to position a marked square from Step 1 on one corner of a 3½" Victoria Floral Blue square. Sew along the drawn line. Trim the outer corner ¼" away from the sewn line, and press towards the blue fabric.

3 Repeat Step 2 positioning a marked square from Step 1 in the opposite corner, aligning the raw edges. (Fig. 2)

4 Repeat Steps 2–3 to create 40 units.

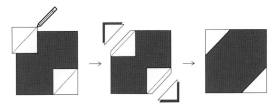

Figure 2 (Make 40)

5 Repeat Steps 2–4 to make an additional 40 units referencing Figure 3 for positioning to ensure the directionality of the fabric is maintained.

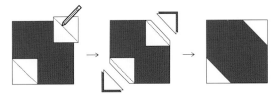

Figure 3 (Make 40)

6 Repeat Steps 2–5 using the 3½" Kew Trellis Blue squares. (Figs. 4 & 5)

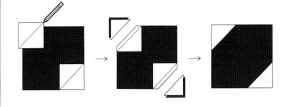

Figure 4 (Make 24)

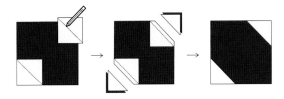

Figure 5 (Make 24)

7 Referencing Figure 6 for placement, attach one snowball unit from Step 4 and one from Step 5 on either side of a 1½" × 3½" rectangle of Oxford Fern Cream. Press towards the snowball units. Repeat to make 40 units.

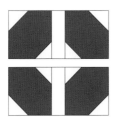

Figure 6 (Make 40)

8 Repeat Step 7 with the snowball units from Step 6 to make 24 units. (Fig. 7)

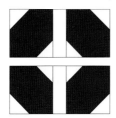

Figure 7 (Make 24)

ASSEMBLING THE FLOWER BLOCKS

1 Referencing Figure 8, join together two assembled Victoria Floral Blue units from Step 9 to either side of a 1½" × 7½" strip of Oxford Fern Cream. Press towards the snowball units. This block will measure 7½" square.

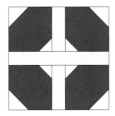

Figure 8 (Make 20)

2 Repeat Step 1 with the 24 Kew Trellis Blue snowball units. (Fig. 9)

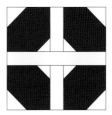

Figure 9 (Make 12)

3 Using the 1⅝" circle template (see page 211), trace 20 circles onto the shiny side of the double-sided fusible web. Following the manufacturer's instructions, fuse onto the wrong side of the Kona Kumquat Orange fabric and cut around the papers.

> **TIP:** *If you prefer to hand-appliqué each circle, just leave ⅛–¼" around the paper for each circle using regular paper instead of double sided fusible for your template.*

4 Peel off the backing paper and fuse each circle onto the centre of the assembled Flower Block featuring the Victoria Floral Blue flowers. Secure with a satin stitch around the circle edge. If using a machine, adjust the stitch width to 3.0 and stitch length of 0.8 or appliqué by hand. (Fig. 10)

Figure 10 (Make 20)

> **TIP:** *To maintain a smooth circle when satin stitching by machine, pause with the needle down on the outside edge of the circle before adjusting the position of the fabrics. Repeat at regular intervals and stitch slowly.*

5 Repeat Steps 3–4 but with the Kew Trellis Blue snowball units and using Kona Citrus Yellow for the 12 circles. (Fig. 11)

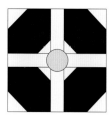

Figure 11 (Make 12)

ASSEMBLING THE QUILT TOP

1 Using the Centre Assembly Diagram as a reference, assemble eight rows of seven blocks each, alternating between the Flower Blocks and the Stripe Blocks, being sure to pay attention to fabrics and stripe orientation. Press the rows in alternate directions and sew together.

2 Using the Border Chart for reference, for the longer borders, join two WOF strips together using a diagonal seam (see page 188) and trim to the size indicated. To make the smaller border strips, cut one WOF strip in half and attach each half to a full WOF strip length using a diagonal seam before trimming them to size.

3 Referencing the Assembly Diagram, join the longer borders to the left and right of the assembled unit from Step 1. Press towards the border, first attaching the cream, then the blue and finally the fruit border.

BORDER CHART

(2) 1½" × 63½" Oxford Fern Cream border strips

(2) 1½" × 51½" Oxford Fern Cream border strips

(2) 2½" × 65½" Manor Tile Blue border strips

(2) 2½"× 55½" Manor Tile Blue border strips

(2) 3½" × 69½" Conservatory Fruits Yellow border strips

(2) 3½" × 61½" Conservatory Fruits Yellow border strips

BACKING

Cut the Hidcote Berry Blue into 2 WOF × 72" long rectangles and join them together on the long side. This will allow an overhang around the quilt top to accommodate any movement while you are quilting.

> **TIP:** *If you are sending your top out to be professionally quilted by someone using a long arm machine, be sure to check that you are supplying their required amount of additional fabric around the quilt top. Most long arm quilters have a minimum, so it's best to check before cutting.*

QUILTING

Stile was quilted using a Rennie Mackintosh rose pattern to complement the Art Nouveau design. A simple, free-motion design would also work well on the Flower Blocks with a leafy trellis in the borders.

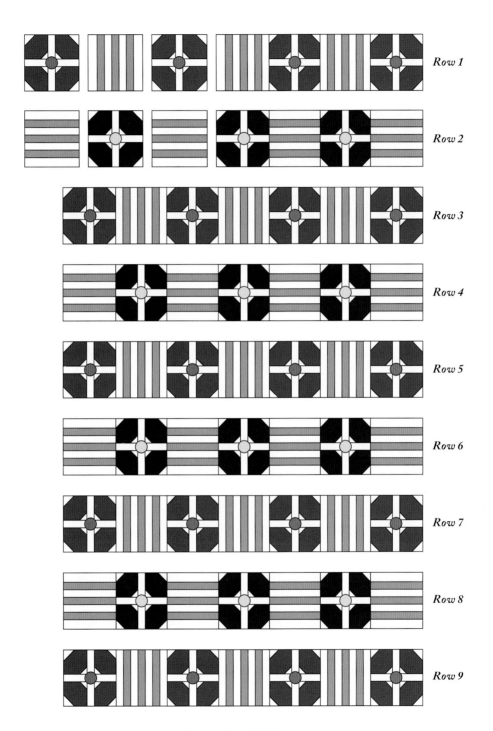

Row 1

Row 2

Row 3

Row 4

Row 5

Row 6

Row 7

Row 8

Row 9

Centre Assembly Diagram

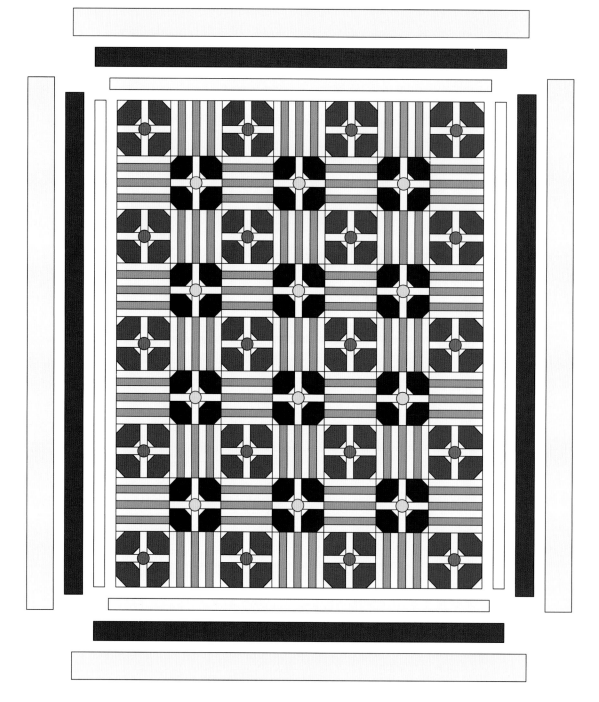

Assembly Diagram

ALTERNATE COLOURWAY

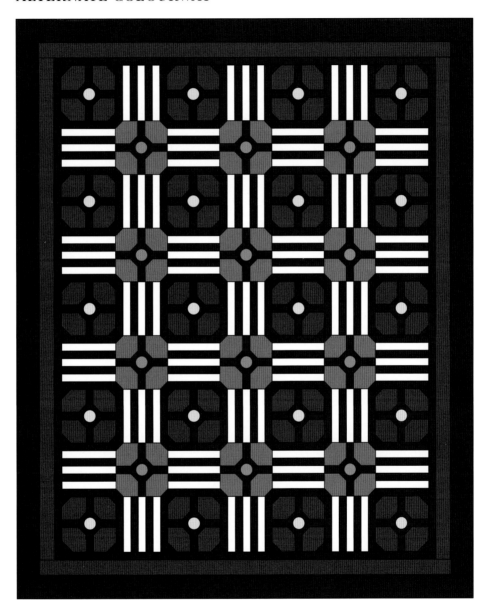

This version of Stile combines red flowers, yellow and green centres.
The striking dark background fabric creates a dramatic feel.

Conservatory Fruits

MERTON

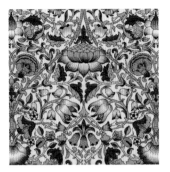

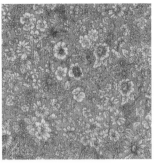

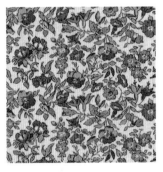

From top: Lodden, Emily Silhouette, Mamie

Merton Abbey is the name of the printing works bought by Liberty in 1904, located in London on the River Wandle. In the early period, wooden blocks were hand carved and then used on a variety of fabrics by an impressive team of over 50 skilled artisans.

During this same period, strippy quilts were popular, especially in the North of England. As the men at Merton printed fine motifs onto fabrics, the women in mining communities close to Durham, hand-stitched designs onto simply-pieced quilts mounted on frames in their homes. This creative enterprise was backed by the Rural Industries Bureau and the finished quilts were sold by exclusive London retailers, including Liberty.

Merton is a celebration of these historically significant crafts. Our everyday lives have changed dramatically in the past one hundred years, but the pleasure that can be derived from creating slowly with our hands, has certainly not diminished.

The simple, traditional layout of this quilt really allows the Liberty fabric to shine and it is the perfect pattern for combining two prints that you love. I chose this rich yellow print called Emily Silhouette, from the first Liberty quilting collection, The English Garden. Along with the Wiltshire Shade Cream cotton, they provide a nod to traditional strip quilts and make the quilting stand out. The Wiltshire Shade is also a really versatile blender and so useful in your stash. The Lasenby Cotton is lovely to handle, which takes me on to the hand quilting on Merton.

I wanted to create a quilting template that truly reflects the spirit of the Art and Crafts Movement, so the shapes have been inspired by the Liberty Print, Lodden. Not only is this a Liberty Classic I love, it also works perfectly as it was originally designed by William Morris in 1884. His studio was just down the road from the Merton Print Works! My aim was to keep the quilting simple, but the shapes allow for embellishment and more details could be added.

My final nod to the past is binding Merton in the traditional English way, which is turning in the raw edges to create a knife-edge or butted finish. It works so well in this design because it allows the strips to continue to the very edges of the quilt.

MERTON

Finished Quilt Size: 70" × 80"

MATERIALS

Wiltshire Shade Cream: 2¼ yards (2.06 m) (must be one continuous length)

Emily Silhouette Yellow: 2¼ yards (2.06 m) (must be one continuous length)

Mamie Pink: 4¾ yards (4.34 m) for the backing

Batting: 78" × 88" (1.98 m × 2.24 m)

Templates (see pages 216 & 217)

Fine chalk pencil

Cotton basting thread

Hand quilting thread (I used Aurifil 12-wt Gold 2975 and 12-wt Cream 2026)

Hand quilting needle

Thimble

TIP: *I recommend using a chalk pencil to transfer the quilting designs onto the stripes in Merton, but feel free to use your favourite transfer method. Consider using a tracing wheel or plastic stencil and pounce chalk, a hera marker or even a lightweight, tearaway quilting paper.*

CUTTING

From the Wiltshire Shade Cream, cut:

(3) 10½" × 81" strips

From the Emily Silhouette Yellow cut:

(2) 11" × 81" strips

(2) 10½" × 81" strips

NOTE: *Cut the Emily Silhouette Yellow 11" x 81" strips into the selvedge as needed. The quilt has a knife edge binding and the extra width will be turned in and allows the finish to have the same size strips.*

ASSEMBLING THE QUILT TOP

1 Referencing the Assembly Diagram, pin and sew together five alternating strips of 10½" wide Wiltshire Shade Cream and Emily Silhouette Yellow with right sides together to creatre the centre of the quilt. With the wrong side facing up, press the seams towards the Emily Silhouette Yellow fabric, then turn to the right side and press again to ensure the strips lay flat.

2 Add an 11" wide strip of Yellow to either long side of the assembled unit from Step 1, taking care to position the selvedge edges on the outside edge of the pieced top, and press in the same manner.

TIP: *When quilt tops are simple like Merton, the piecing and the pressing need to be as perfect as possible. Every little variance seems to show, so take time to press the top well before moving on to the quilting.*

TRANSFERRING THE QUILTING DESIGN

1 Referencing Figure 1 for placement, position a photocopy of Merton Template A underneath the quilt top and transfer the design onto the yellow fabric strips using a fine chalk pencil. Repeat with Merton Template B onto the cream strips (pages 216 & 217).

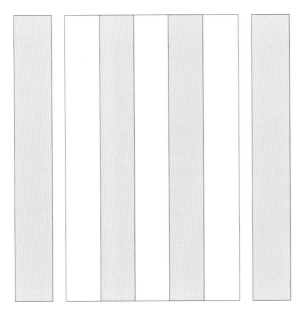

Assembly Diagram

Figure 1

TIP: *A light box will allow the quilt top to remain flat and improve accuracy if you are tracing the templates onto your quilt top. These are relatively inexpensive but your local quilt shop may have one you can use. You also may need a second chalk pencil colour to show up on the pale cream fabric. See the TIP on the facing page for some other suggestions for transferring quilting lines onto your quilt top. Experiment with a few different tools and methods before marking to be sure you have found the method you like. See the Resources on page 222 for some of my favourites.*

BACKING

Cut the Mamie Pink into (2) 85" long strips and join them together on the long side. This will allow an overhang around the quilt top to accommodate any movement that may occur when quilting.

QUILTING

1 Layer the backing wrong side up, with the batting and the quilt top right side up. Baste together the layers using the basting thread.

2 Following the transferred quilting design and starting at the centre of the quilt, begin hand quilting, filling in one strip at a time.

TIP: *When hand quilting, consider using a large quilting hoop or a lap frame to keep the quilt top taut as you work. There are also a variety of needles, thimbles, gloves, clips, thread conditioners and more available to help make the process more enjoyable. If you love this method, take some time to experiment with a few of these. If this is your first hand quilting project, I have kept the supplies minimal, to encourage you to give it a go!*

3 Hand quilt a parallel line ⅛" away from each long seam of the Cream strips.

HOW TO ATTACH A KNIFE-EDGE BINDING

1 With the layers still basted together, trim the batting and backing fabric to the same dimensions as the quilt top.

2 Move the quilt top and backing fabric away from the edges and trim the batting a further ½" away from the quilt top edge being sure not to cut through the fabrics. Repeat around the perimeter of the quilt.

3 Fold the quilt top over the trimmed batting and gently press as you progress.

4 Fold in the backing fabric with the wrong sides facing, gently rolling the fold to align all edges. Press.

> TIP: *Clip the knife-edge fold into place using quilting clips if preferred or consider working on one edge at a time to ensure accuracy.*

5 Use a ladder stitch to join the quilt top and backing fabric at the fold. At the corners fold the fabric to make a mitred join before sewing together. (Fig. 2)

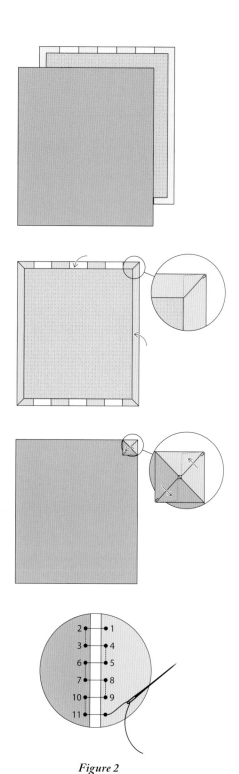

Figure 2

ARGYLL

The Liberty Store stands proudly at the end of Argyll Street, London. I love turning the corner from Oxford Circus station and seeing it before me! It was completed in 1924, sadly after the company's founder Arthur Liberty had passed away. However, he had been very involved with planning what it should look like. Fortunately for us, the building sat just outside the Crown property boundery, which enabled the architects to be considerably more creative than with the adjoining buildings. Next time you visit, notice how the structures next door are so much more conservative.

The mock-Tudor facade was chosen as a deliberate nod to Britain's Elizabethan period, perceived as a time of pioneering, adventure and prosperity. This structure was a brave and bold statement.

The Argyll Quilt alludes to the unforgettable black and white exterior of the store. I have combined Log Cabin and Courthouse Step blocks to mirror the structure of the timber frames and leaded windows which decorate the façade. To add a modern twist to this traditional quilting pattern, I transformed the red centre of the log cabin (which historically alludes to the hearth in a home) into a heart. For me this symbolises that the Liberty Store is the heart of Liberty Fabrics and the spiritual home of Liberty fans worldwide.

This quilt was also designed to showcase Tana Lawn. This exceptional cloth has been sold in Liberty from 1910 and by the time the Store opened, it had become one of Liberty Fabrics' most desired cottons. The Log Cabin strips include classic prints: Strawberry Thief, Lodden, Pepper, Capel and Adelajda. The border fabric is London Fields, and I love the story of how this design came to be. Rather than being an accurate depiction of London, it is actually a culmination of different areas of the city where members of the Design Studio lived.

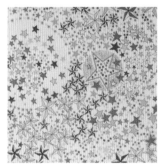

From top: Strawberry Thief, Capel, Adelajda.

ARGYLL

Finished Quilt Size: 50" × 65" • *Finished Block Size:* 7½"

MATERIALS

Oxford Fern Navy: 1½ yards (1.37 m) including the binding

Oxford Fern Cream: 1 yard (91 cm)

Capel Navy: ½ yard (46 cm)

Pepper Green: ⅜ yard (34 cm)

Strawberry Thief Grey: ¼ yard (23 cm)

Adelajda Cream: ⅝ yard (57 cm)

Lodden Grey: ⅜ yard (38 cm)

Capel Grey: ½ yard (46 cm)

Capel Red: ¼ yard (23 cm)

London Fields Blue: ½ yard (46 cm)

Capel Indigo: 2 yards (1.83 m) for the backing

Batting: 58" × 73" (1.47 m × 1.85 m)

Glue pen

8½" or larger square acrylic ruler

CUTTING

From the Oxford Fern Navy, cut:
(2) 8" × 42" strips, subcut into:
   (48) 8" × 1¼" rectangles
   (18) 7¼" × 1¼" rectangles

(2) 6½" × 42" strips, subcut into:
   (48) 6½" × 1¼" rectangles

(6) 2½" x 42" strips for the binding

From the Oxford Fern Cream, cut:
(1) 8" × 42" strip, subcut into:
   (30) 8" × 1¼" rectangles

(1) 7¼" × 42" strip, subcut into:
   (18) 7¼" × 1¼" rectangles
   (12) 5" × 1¼" rectangles

(1) 6½" × 42" strip, subcut into:
   (30) 6½" × 1¼" rectangles

(2) 3½" × 42" strips, subcut into:
   (36) 3½" × 1¼" rectangles
   (24) 2" × 1¼" rectangles

(1) 1¼" × 42" strip, subcut into:
   (24) 1¼" squares
   (6) ⅞" squares

(1) ⅞" × 42" strip, subcut into:
   (42) ⅞" squares

From the Capel Navy, cut:
(1) 6½" × 52" strip, subcut into:
   (18) 6½" × 1¼" rectangles
   (18) 5¾" × 1¼" rectangles

(1) 5" × 52" strip, subcut into:
   (36) 5" × 1¼" rectangles

From the Pepper Green, cut:
(1) 5" × 52" strip, subcut into:
   (18) 5" × 1¼" rectangles
   (18) 4¼" × 1¼" rectangles

(1) 3½" × 52" strip, subcut into:
   (36) 3½" × 1¼" rectangles

From the Strawberry Thief Grey, cut:
(1) 3½" × 52" strip, subcut into:
   (18) 3½" × 1¼" rectangles
   (18) 2¾" × 1¼" rectangles

(1) 2" × 52" strip, subcut into:
   (36) 2" × 1¼" rectangles

From the Adelajda Cream, cut:
(1) 6½" × 52" strip, subcut into:
   (36) 6½" × 1¼" rectangles

(1) 5¾" × 52" strip, subcut into:
   (18) 5¾" × 1¼" rectangles
   (12) 3½" × 1¼" rectangles

(1) 5" × 52½" strip, subcut into:
   (42) 5" × 1¼" rectangles

From the Lodden Grey, cut:
(1) 5" × 52" strip, subcut into:
   (36) 5" × 1¼" rectangles

(1) 4¼" × 52" strip, subcut into:
   (18) 4¼" × 1¼" rectangles
   (18) 3½" × 1¼" rectangles

From the Capel Grey, cut:
(1) 6½" × 52" strip, subcut into:

    (24) 6½" × 1¼" rectangles

    (12) 5" × 1¼" rectangles

(1) 3½" × 52" strip, subcut into:

    (36) 3½" × 1¼" rectangles

(1) 2¾" × 52" strip, subcut into:

    (18) 2¾" × 1¼" rectangles

    (18) 2" × 1¼" rectangles

From the Capel Red, cut:
(2) 2" × 52" strips, subcut into:

    (36) 2" squares

    (24) 2" × 1¼" rectangles

From the London Fields Blue, cut: (5) 3" × 52" strips

ASSEMBLING LOG CABIN BLOCK 1

NOTE: *Always press towards the most recently added strip unless stated otherwise.*

1 Referencing Figure 1 and starting with the 2" Capel Red square, add the rectangle logs in the following order, working in a counter-clockwise direction and always pressing towards the most recently added strip:

    2" Capel Grey rectangle

    2¾" Capel Grey rectangle

    2¾" Strawberry Thief Grey rectangle

    3½" Strawberry Thief Grey rectangle

2 Using a square ruler, check that the unit measures 3½" square and trim any excess if necessary. Continue by adding:

    3½" Lodden Grey rectangle

    4¼" Lodden Grey rectangle

    4¼" Pepper Green rectangle

    5" Pepper Green rectangle

3 Using a square ruler, check that the unit measures 5" square and trim any excess as necessary. Continue by adding:

    5" Adelajda Cream rectangle

    5¾" Adelajda Cream rectangle

    5¾" Capel Navy rectangle

    6½" Capel Navy rectangle

4 Using a square ruler, check that the unit measures 6½" square and trim any unecessary excess. Continue by adding:

    6½" Oxford Fern Cream rectangle

    7¼" Oxford Fern Cream rectangle

    7¼" Oxford Fern Navy rectangle

    8" Oxford Fern Navy rectangle

5 Using a square ruler, check that the unit measures 8" square and trim off any excess if necessary.

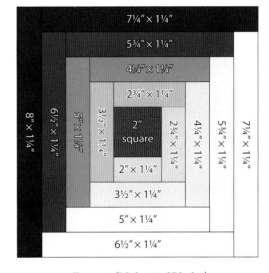

Figure 1 (Make 18 of Block 1)

6 Repeat to create a total of 18 of Block 1.

ASSEMBLING COURTHOUSE STEPS HEART BLOCK 2

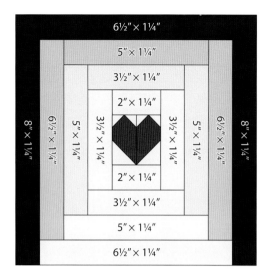

Figure 2

ASSEMBLING THE HEART CENTRE

1 Position (1) 1¼" Oxford Fern Cream square onto the bottom of (1) 2" × 1¼" Capel Red rectangle. Referencing Figure 3 for directionality and using a chalk pencil, draw a diagonal line on the wrong side of the square. Sew along the drawn line. Trim away the excess fabric ¼" away from the sewn line and press towards the lighter fabric.

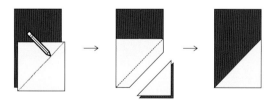

Figure 3

2 Position (1) ⅞" Oxford Fern Cream square onto the top right corner of the unit from Step 1. Draw a diagonal line on the wrong side of the square. Sew along the drawn line. Trim off any excess fabric ¼" away from the sewn line and press towards the lighter fabric. (Fig. 4)

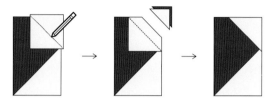

Figure 4

TIP: *Use a glue pen to hold the ⅞" square in place by applying a small amount in the top outside corner; it will then be cut away after sewing.*

3 Repeat Step 2 with another ⅞" Oxford Fern Cream square, this time positioning it in the top left corner of the unit from Step 2 and set aside. (Fig. 5)

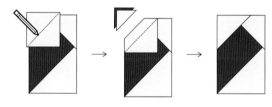

Figure 5

4 To make the opposite side of the heart, repeat Step 1 referencing Figure 6 for directionality of the drawn line.

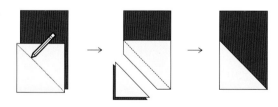

Figure 6

5 Repeat Steps 2–3 with the unit from Step 4. (Fig. 7)

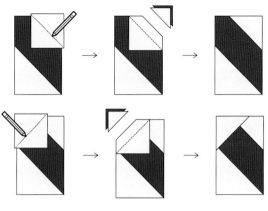

Figure 7

6 Sew together the units created in Steps 3 and 5 to create the heart shape (Fig. 8). Press the seam open.

Figure 8 (Make 12)

7 Using a square ruler, check that the unit measures 2" square and trim any excess if necessary. Repeat to make 12 heart units.

ADDING THE STEPS

Attach the rectangle steps to a Heart unit. Sew the first pair of rectangles on the top and bottom, the second pair on the sides, and so forth, pressing after each addition.

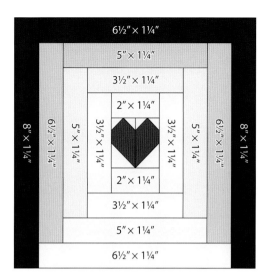

Figure 9

Steps 1 and 2: 2" Oxford Fern Cream rectangles

Steps 3 and 4: 3½" Oxford Fern Cream rectangles

Using a square ruler, check that the unit measures 3½" square and trim any excess if necessary.

Step 5: 3½" Adelajda Cream rectangle

Step 6: 3½" Oxford Fern Cream rectangle

Steps 7 and 8: 5" Adelajda Cream rectangles

Using a square ruler, check that the unit measures 5" square and trim any excess.

Step 9: 5" Capel Grey rectangle

Step 10: 5" Oxford Fern Cream rectangle

Steps 11–12: 6½" Capel Grey rectangles

Using a square ruler, check that the unit measures 6½" square and trim off any excess.

Step 13: 6½" Oxford Fern Navy rectangle

Step 14: 6½" Oxford Fern Cream rectangle

Steps 15 and 16: 8" Oxford Fern Navy rectangles
   Using a square ruler, check that the unit measures 8" square and trim any excess.
   Repeat to make a total of 12 blocks.

ASSEMBLING COURTHOUSE STEPS BLOCK 3

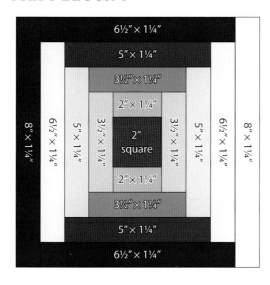

Figure 10 (Make 6 of Block 3)

Attach the rectangle steps to a 2" Capel Red square. Sew the first pair on the top and bottom, the second pair on the sides and so forth, pressing after each addition.

Steps 1 and 2: 2" Strawberry Thief Grey rectangles

Steps 3 and 4: 3½" Capel Grey rectangles
   Using a square ruler, check that the unit measures 3½" square and trim off excess.

Steps 5 and 6: 3½" Pepper Green rectangles

Steps 7 and 8: 5" Lodden Grey rectangles
   Using a square ruler, check that the unit measures 5" square and trim away any excess.

Steps 9 and 10: 5" Capel Navy rectangles

Steps 11 and 12: 6½" Adelajda Cream rectangles
   Using a square ruler, check that the unit measures 6½" square and trim any excess.

Steps 13 and 14: 6½" Oxford Fern Navy rectangles

Step 15: 8" Oxford Fern Cream rectangle

Step 16: 8" Oxford Fern Navy rectangle
   Using a square ruler, check that the unit measures 8" square and trim off.

   Repeat to make a total of 6 blocks.

ASSEMBLING COURTHOUSE STEPS BLOCK 4

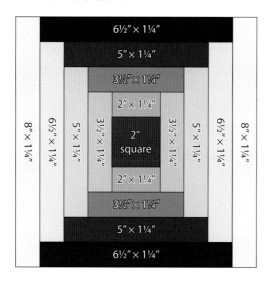

Figure 11 *(Make 12 of Block 4)*

1 Repeat the step additions as in Assembling Block 3, but replace Step 16 with an 8" Oxford Fern Cream rectangle.

2 Repeat to make a total of 12 blocks.

ASSEMBLING THE QUILT TOP

1 Referencing the Assembly Diagram, sew the assembled blocks into eight rows of six squares each, pressing the seams in alternate directions for each row.

Rows 1, 4 and 5: Sew together 6 Log Cabin Block 1 squares.

Rows 2 and 3: Sew together 6 Heart Block squares.

Rows 6, 7 and 8: Sew together four Block 4 squares attaching a Block 3 square to both ends of each row.

2 Sew the rows together, pressing the seams downwards after each addition.

3 Cut (1) 3" London Fields Blue strip in half. Join one of these half strips to a WOF 3" strip using a diagonal seam (see page 188). Trim to 60½". Repeat to make another 60½" border strip.

4 Trim (1) 3" London Fields Blue strip to 50½". Repeat to make another 50½" border strip.

5 Join the longer borders to the left and right of the assembled unit from Step 2 and press towards the borders. Join the shorter borders to the top and bottom, again pressing towards the border.

QUILTING

Argyll has been machine quilted by creating a square midway inside every block, with three rows of quilting on the London Fields Blue border. This was intended to convey the look of the windows on the façade of the Liberty of London Department Store.

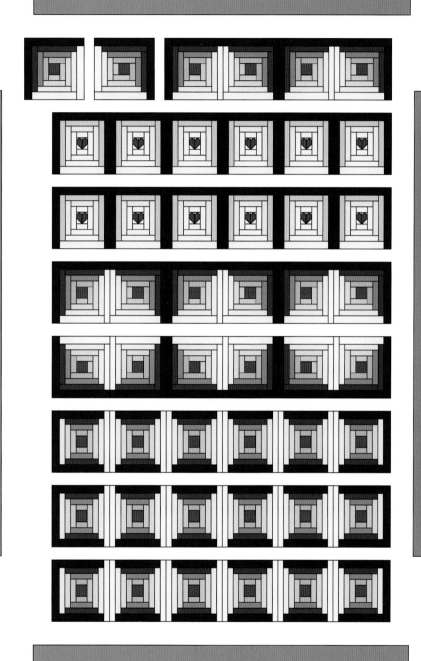

Assembly Diagram

DISCOVERY

It's incredible to know that the timbers from two old and decommissioned British Navy training ships were used to construct the Liberty interior. In fact, the Store's frontage is said to match Navy Ship HMS Hindustan in both height and length. This is a clever and perhaps eccentric interpretation of Arthur Liberty's vision to dock a ship in the centre of London and may also be why many fabric lovers refer to the store as 'the mothership'.

The oak atriums, wood-carved staircases and fireplaces give a very warm and homely feel to visitors and reflect a genuine admiration of skilled craftsmanship — shipbuilders and carpenters alike. Perhaps that is why makers feel so comfortable there too.

I chose to tell the incredible story of the Hindustan by creating a nautical theme. A Mariner's Compass sits at the centre of this quilt, set inside Storm at Sea blocks which cleverly give the illusion of waves, even though all the seams are straight. (I don't know how this works but it's very clever.) Beyond the sea is a starry night sky by which to navigate.

I hope the design inspires you to undertake a quilting adventure of your own and venture into the world of Foundation Paper Piecing (FPP). Discovery is about embracing the unknown, and the construction of this quilt is certainly achievable once broken down into sections. In fact, repeating the Storm at Sea blocks is a brilliant way to build confidence, and the accuracy you achieve with FPP is perfect for the points of the compass.

From top: Wiltshire Shade, Fruit Silhouette, Primula Dawn.

The fabrics I selected are Fruit Silhouette in Yellow, Aqua, Pink and Blue from Liberty's Orchard Garden Quilting Collection. The colour saturation is really striking and gives the dramatic effect I wanted set against the Blue and Cream Wiltshire Shade blenders.

DISCOVERY

Finished Quilt Size: 64" square • *Finished Block Sizes:* 24", 12" and 8"

MATERIALS

Wiltshire Shade Blue:
5⅛ yards (4.68 m) including the binding

Wiltshire Shade Cream:
½ yard (46 cm)

Fruit Silhouette Yellow:
1⅛ yards (1.03 m)

Fruit Silhouette Pink:
⅝ yard (57 cm)

Fruit Silhouette Blue:
2¾ yards (2.51 m)

Fruit Silhouette Aqua:
½ yard (46 cm)

Primula Dawn Coral: 4 yards (3.66 m) for the backing

Batting: 72" × 72" (1.83 m × 1.83 m)

Templates (see pages 207–212)

CUTTING

From the Wiltshire Shade Blue, cut:

(1) 13" × 42" strip, subcut into (4) Unit (C)

(5) 10" × 42" strips, subcut into:
    (48) 10" squares, subcut each into:
        4 equal triangles making a total of 192 triangles (G2, G3)

(5) 6" × 42" strips, subcut into:
    (16) 6" squares, subcut each into:

2 triangles making a total of 32 triangles (H2, H3)

(12) 6" squares, subcut each into:
    4 equal triangles making a total of 48 triangles (F2, F3, F4, F5)

(2) 4" × 42" strips, subcut into:
    (4) 4" × 14" rectangles (B6)

(4) 3½" × 42" strips, subcut into:
    (48) 3½" squares subcut each into:
        4 equal triangles making a total of 192 triangles (D2, D3, D4, D5)

(12) 3" × 42" strips, subcut into:
    (96) 3" × 5" rectangles, subcut into:
        (48) rectangles, subcut into two triangles on the diagonal one way (E2, E4)
        (48) rectangles subcut into two triangles on the diagonal in the opposite direction (E3, E5), making a total of 192 triangles

(7) 2½" × 42" strips for the binding

From the Wiltshire Shade Cream, cut:

(2) 4" × 42" strips, subcut into:
    (4) 14" × 4" rectangles (A6)

(1) 3" × 42" strip, subcut into:
    (4) 10" × 3" rectangles (B5)

(2) 2½" × 42" strip, subcut into:
    (8) 8" × 2½" rectangles (A1, B1)

From the Fruit Silhouette Yellow, cut:

(2) 8" × 42" strips, subcut into:
    (16) 8" × 3" rectangles (H1)
    (18) 4" × 3" rectangles (G1)

(3) 5" × 42" strips, subcut into:
    (16) 7" × 5" rectangles (A3, A4, B3, B4)

(1) 4" × 42" strip, subcut into:
    (14) 4" × 3" rectangles (G1)

From the Fruit Silhouette Pink, cut:

(1) 10" × 42" strip, subcut into:
    (2) 10" × 3" rectangles (A5)
    (4) 8" × 2½" rectangles (A2, B2)
    (4) 4" x 3" rectangles (G1)

(2) 4" × 42" strips, subcut into:

    (28) 4" x 3" rectangles (G1)

From the Fruit Silhouette Blue, cut:

(3) 8" × 42" strips, subcut into:

    (12) 8" squares, subcut each into:

        4 equal triangles making a total of 48 triangles (F6, F7, F8, F9) and

    (12) 4" squares (F1)

(6) 4½" × 42" strips, subcut into:

    (48) 4½" squares, subcut each diagonally into:

        4 equal triangles making a total of 192 triangles (D6, D7, D8, D9)

(8) 4" × 42" strips, subcut into:

    (48) 4" × 7" rectangles (E1)

(3) 2½" × 42" strips, subcut into:

    (48) 2½" squares (D1)

From the Fruit Silhouette Aqua, cut:

(1) 10" × 42" strip, subcut into:

    (2) 10" × 3" rectangles (A5)

    (4) 8" × 2½" rectangles (A2, B2)

    (18) 4" × 3" rectangles (G1)

(1) 4" × 42" strip, subcut into:
    (14) 4" × 3" rectangles (G1)

ASSEMBLING THE CENTRAL COMPASS

1 Photocopy the paper piecing patterns on pages 208–212.

2 Referencing Figures 1a and 1b, Foundation Paper Piece (FPP, ref p191) all the individual sections, using a stitch length of 1.8mm. Make two Compass quarters as shown in Figure 1a and two as shown in Figure 1b noting the different colour order.

3 Join one Unit A to one Unit B. Press the seam to one side.

4 Using the template on page 208, cut (4) of concave Unit C from the C strip. Position Unit C on top of the unit from Step 3. Pin and sew. Press towards Unit C. (Fig. 1)

5 Repeat Steps 2–4 to create the remaining three quarters of the Central Compass.

6 Join the top two quarters and press towards the B6.

7 Join the bottom two quarters and press towards B6.

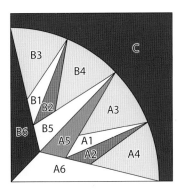

Figure 1a

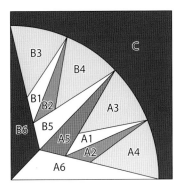

Figure 1b

8 Join the top and bottom halves, nesting the seams at the centre point. (Fig. 2)

Figure 2

9 Remove the papers and press well.

TIP: *When joining the sections of the compass, set the stitch length to 5.0 and sew. Check that the points are accurately matched and if no adjustment is necessary, go back over the line at the normal stitch length. It is much easier to unpick a longer stitch length!*

ASSEMBLING THE STORM AT SEA BLOCKS

1 Photocopy the templates on pages 209, 210 and 212. You will need 48 copies of Template D, 48 copies of Template E and 12 copies of Template F to create a total of 12 Storm at Sea Blocks.

2 Foundation Paper Piece the individual sections using the cut fabrics listed in the Cutting instructions to ensure proper fabric placement.

3 Working with one block at a time, join an assembled Unit D to either side of one Unit E. Press towards Unit D. Repeat.

4 Join an assembled Unit E to either side of one Unit F. Press towards Unit F.

5 Join the rows created in Steps 3 and 4 to make one Storm at Sea block.

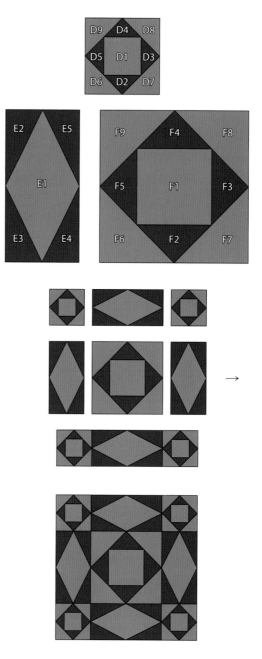

Figure 3 (Make 12 Storm at Sea Blocks)

6 Repeat Steps 3–5 to make a total of 12 Storm at Sea Blocks.

7 Remove the papers and press.

ASSEMBLING THE STAR BLOCKS

1 Photocopy the templates on pages 211 and 212. You will need 96 copies of Template G and 16 copies of Template H.

2 Foundation Paper Piece the individual sections using the cut fabrics listed in the Cutting instructions to ensure proper fabric placement. You will need 32 copies of Template G for each small star colour. (Fig. 4)

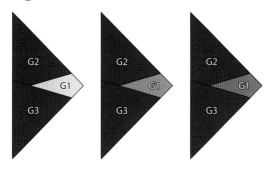

Figure 4

3 Working with one block and colour at a time, join two units together and press to the left.

4 Join another two units together and press to the right.

5 Join the units from Steps 3–4 being sure to nest the seams.

6 Repeat Steps 3–5 to make a total of 8 Small Yellow Stars (Fig. 5), 8 Aqua Stars (Fig. 6), 8 Pink Stars (Fig. 7), and 4 Large Yellow Stars (Fig. 8).

7 Remove the papers and press each block well.

Figure 5 (Make 8 Small Yellow Stars)

Figure 6 (Make 8 Aqua Stars)

Figure 7 (Make 8 Pink Stars)

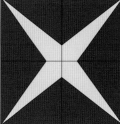

Figure 8 (Make 4 Large Yellow Stars)

ASSEMBLING THE QUILT TOP

1 Join together two assembled Storm at Sea Blocks. Press and then repeat.

2 Join four Storm at Sea Blocks together and press. Repeat to create two rows of four blocks each.

3 Join the blocks from Step 1 to either side of the Central Compass and press away from the Compass.

4 Join the rows created in Step 2 to the top and bottom of the assembled unit from Step 3. Press away from the Compass and set aside.

5 Join the Small Star Blocks in the following order and repeat, to make a total of four rows of six blocks each:

pink + yellow + aqua + pink + yellow + aqua

6 Sew a Large Yellow Star Block to both ends of two assembled rows from Step 5. Press well.

7 Pin the borders from Step 5 to the left and right of the assembled unit from Step 4, aligning the centre point. Sew and press outwards.

8 Pin the longer borders from Step 6 to the top and bottom of the assembled unit from Step 7, aligning the centre point. Press outwards.

CUTTING THE BACKING FABRIC

Cut the Primula Dawn into two strips, each 72" long. Join them together on the long side. This will allow an overhang around the quilt top to accommodate any movement when quilting.

QUILTING

Discovery has been professionally long arm quilted to recall the rolling waves of the sea on the Storm at Sea Blocks and highlight the piecing details of the Star Blocks and Central Compass. This would be a great quilt to practice different free-motion quilting patterns upon due to the intricate piecing and busy fabrics. For Discovery, the focus will likely remain on the piecing and overall design so the quilting can simply add texture and movement where desired.

Assembly Diagram

I n the 1930s, the development of screen printing introduced exciting opportunities for Liberty. Screens were more time-efficient to produce than woodblocks, and the level of detail that could be achieved was exciting.

The company was also now wholesaling fabric to other shops and demand for all base cloths, but in particular Tana Lawn, was high.

Betsy is a stylised small floral design which dates from 1933 and its place in the heart of Liberty fans is confirmed by the fact that it is one of the best-selling fabrics of all time. It is so well-loved, it was the pattern selected to adorn part of the exterior of the Liberty Store facing Carnaby Street in 2009.

An intriguing detail, seen in other prints of this time, is the fine broken line which surrounds the flower petals. Developments in print technology made this delicate transfer of original drawings possible, and certainly added to its charm.

Meadow was created to celebrate the simple beauty of Betsy and to showcase how the stunning colourways available on Tana Lawn can work together in harmony.

The soft curved appliqué shapes allude to details from the fabric design itself and can be arranged in a variety of ways with as many appliqué elements as you like. I chose to needle-turn all of my raw edges for this quilt, but you could also use raw-edge appliqué if you prefer.

I also decided to fussy cut motifs from Betsy fabrics in the different sized flowers to add another level of interest to the design. On a practical level, this keeps all of my different sized shapes in the correct order as well!

The background fabric is Essex Linen. The slightly rougher texture of this cloth provides an interesting contrast to the silky-smooth Tana Lawn and sets off the fresh, bright colours of Betsy.

I know Betsy exists in extensive colourways and that the Meadow shapes can be used in many combinations as well, especially if you assemble the shapes on a large background square instead of making smaller blocks for the centre of the quilt. I cannot wait to see how you personalise your Meadow!

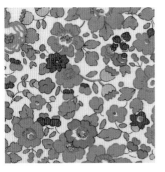
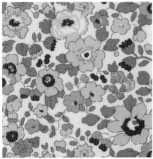
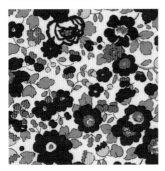

From top, Betsy Green, Betsy Grey, Betsy Red.

MEADOW

Finished Quilt Size: 42½" square • *Finished Block Size:* 5½"

MATERIALS

Essex Linen Charcoal:
1½ yards (1.37 m)

Betsy Red: 1 yard (91 cm)

Betsy Blue: ½ yard (46 cm)

Betsy Yellow: ½ yard
(46 cm)

Betsy Green: ½ yard (46 cm)

Betsy Grey: ½ yard (46 cm)

Betsy Red: ½ yard (46 cm) for
the binding

Batting: 48" × 48"
(1.22 m × 1.22m)

Templates (see page 215)

Freezer Paper

Square Ruler at least 6½"

Appliqué pins

PREPARATION

Using the patterns on page
215, create templates of the
appliqué shapes. Transfer
5 large flowers, 10 medium
flowers and 10 small flowers
onto freezer paper and cut
along the drawn lines.

CUTTING

*From the Essex Linen
Charcoal, cut:*

(5) 6½" × 42" strips, subcut
into:

    (25) 6½" squares

    (1) 6" × 28" rectangle

(3) 6" × 42" strips, subcut
into:

    (2) 6" × 39" rectangles

    (1) 6" × 28" rectangle

TIP: *Cut the background
squares larger than needed.
Thus, any fraying caused by
handling the fabric during
the appliqué process, can be
trimmed away at the end.*

From the Betsy Red, cut:

(1) 11½" × 48" rectangle

(8) 2½" × 52" strips, subcut
into:

    (2) 2½" × 43" rectangles

    (2) 2½" × 39" rectangles

    Reserve the remaining (4)
    strips for the binding.

From the remaining fabric,
position 1 Large, 2 Medium
and 2 Small Flower freezer
paper templates onto the
right side of the fabric, fussy

cutting if desired. Cut around
each shape leaving a ¼" seam
allowance if using needle-
turn appliqué.

*From the Betsy Blue, Yellow
and Green fabrics cut:*

(1) 9" × 48" rectangle for the
backing

From the remaining fabrics,
position 1 Large, 2 Medium
and 2 Small Flower freezer
paper templates onto the
right side of the fabric, fussy
cutting if desired. Cut around
each shape leaving a ¼" seam
allowance if using needle-
turn appliqué.

From the Betsy Grey, cut:

(1) 11½" × 48" rectangle for
the backing

From the remaining fabric,
position 1 Large, 2 Medium
and 2 Small Flower freezer
paper templates onto the
right side of the fabric, fussy
cutting if desired. Cut around
each shape leaving a ¼" seam
allowance if using needle-
turn appliqué.

TIP: *See page 189 for a refresher
of the needle-turn appliqué
technique.*

ASSEMBLING THE BLOCKS

1 Pin one flower head onto an Essex Linen Charcoal 6½" square using appliqué pins and following the placement guide (Fig. 1). This is for finished appliqué motifs without seam allowances.

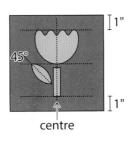

Make 5

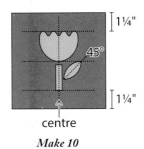

Make 10

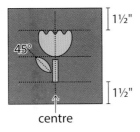

Figure 1 (Make 10)

2 Snip carefully into the concave curves, and needle turn appliqué around the shape. (Fig. 2)

3 Pin one stem beneath the flower head and sew in place. Fold the sides under as you approach each corner. This will create a neat edge. (Fig. 3)

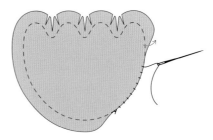

Figure 2

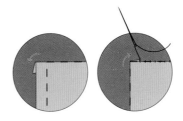

Figure 3

4 Referencing Figure 1, pin one leaf to either the right or left side of the stem and sew in place. At the points of the leaf fold, a horizontal line under first, then fold each side under to make a neat point.

5 Repeat Steps 1–4 to make a total of 25 Flower Blocks. You will need 5 large, 10 medium and 10 small.

6 Using a square ruler, trim the blocks to make 6" squares.

ASSEMBLING THE QUILT TOP

1 Referencing the Assembly Diagram for colour placement, pin and sew together five rows of five blocks each.

2 Join the shorter Essex Linen Charcoal border strips to the left and right-hand sides of the unit from Step 1, and press towards the border.

3 Repeat Step 2, adding the longer Essex Linen Charcoal border strips to the top and bottom.

4 Repeat Steps 2–3 with the Betsy Red strips.

BACKING

Referencing Figure 4, join the backing strips in the following order:

Betsy Red, Blue, Yellow, Green, Grey. Press the seams in one direction. Match the middle point of the backing and the middle point of the quilt top when basting and ensure the backing strips run horizontally.

Figure 4

QUILTING

Meadow has been machine quilted in simple straight lines to avoid stitching over the hand appliqué. Hand quilting would also look beautiful and would not be too onerous on a quilt this size.

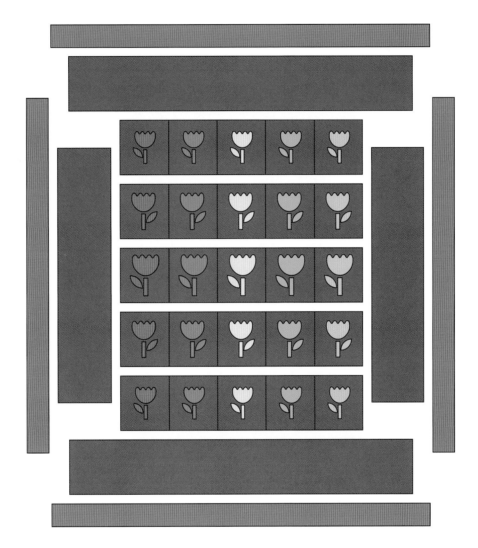

Assembly Diagram

ECLECTIC

When war broke out in 1939, the Liberty print works at Merton was converted to manufacturing aircraft components. Production of fabrics decreased, yet the nation was still very busy stitching.

The 'Make Do and Mend' scheme was a government backed initiative in Wartime Britain to encourage everyone to repair and revive worn-out fabrics and to be thrifty. A booklet with practical guidelines instructed people to create decorative patches and utilise them to cover holes. Quilts as functional objects provided comfort and warmth and were also stitched by wounded soldiers whilst they were recuperating.

In the spirit of quilting with the fabrics one has to hand, I developed the concept for my Eclectic Quilt. I recycled several of my husband's shirts and combined these with small pieces of Liberty Tana Lawn which I had collected over many years, including a vintage piece of Liberty shirting. Off-cuts of batting were used within each square so that you quilt-as-you-go and there is zero waste.

One amazing attribute of Liberty Fabrics is that they work so well in myriad combinations. The eclectic nature of the prints enables the maker to mix and match scale, colour and pattern. I pieced the individual squares and then played with the position of each one until I found a layout that worked on both sides, because the other great thing about this quilt is that it is reversible! Individual patches alternate with shirting on one side, and those on the other side have a small border to frame each of the fabrics.

The best part about this design is that the outer edges of Eclectic do not need to be bound as the raw edges are enclosed in each square. This means that Eclectic can be gradually added to over the years, transforming it from a baby quilt into a king-size one as your Liberty collection increases and more shirts need to be recycled. Of course, this can also feature those treasured small squares of fabrics that you have collected over time.

Why not use the shirts of a loved one and turn this into a memory project?

From top: Ciara, Queue for the Zoo, Patsy

ECLECTIC

Finished Quilt Size: 45" square • *Finished Block Size:* 4½"

MATERIALS	Coordinating thread to match the shirting (this is visible on the finished quilt)	From the Cotton shirts, cut: (100) 6" squares
Liberty Tana Lawn: (100) 6" (15 cm) squares		*From the Batting, cut:* (100) 4½" squares
Five or six Cotton shirts or (12) fat quarters	**CUTTING**	
Batting: 45" × 45" (1.22 m × 1.22 m)	*From the Liberty Tana Lawn, cut:*	
Point Turner	(100) 6" squares	

ASSEMBLING THE BLOCKS

1 Position one 4½" batting square in the centre of the wrong side of (1) 6" shirt square. Sew two diagonal lines to create a cross, securing the lines of stitching at each end. (Fig. 1)

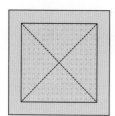

Figure 1

2 Position a Liberty Tana Lawn 6" square right sides together with the shirt and batting square from Step 1. Pin and sew around the edges leaving a gap of 1" on the bottom edge. Trim the corners at a 45-degree angle and turn through. Poke out the corners using a point turner. Press. (Fig. 2)

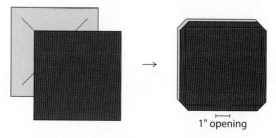

1" opening

Figure 2

3 Close the gap using a ladder stitch (see page 68).

4 Repeat Steps 1–3 to make a total of 100 blocks.

ASSEMBLING THE QUILT TOP

1 Arrange the units in rows of 10, alternating which side is visible — the shirt or the Liberty print.

TIP: *If you are using more than one shirt fabric, arrange the squares to create an interesting pattern if desired.*

2 It is important to check that the arrangement works from both sides as the quilt is reversible. I recommend working on a flat surface or a design wall and taking a picture of one side, then flipping each square over and taking a second picture. The side that is showing at this point will become the unframed side of the quilt.

> TIP: *Take time to play with different arrangements before sewing. Bear in mind that certain Liberty prints could work really well within the frame created by the seams. You can create movement in the quilt top through colour placement or by playing with patterns in the different shirt designs.*

3 Join two blocks together by using a ½" seam allowance, backstitching at the beginning and end of each seam. Continue adding blocks along the row in the same way. Press the seams open.

4 Repeat Step 3 to join all the rows. (Fig. 3)

5 Position Rows 1 and 2 right sides together, match the seams and use sewing clips to secure them. Sew together with a ½" seam allowance. Press the seam open.

> TIP: *Because this quilt is reversible, it can be challenging to keep track of which side is which. I recommend placing a pin on the right side of each of the assembled rows before attaching them to help you keep track.*

6 Repeat Step 5 to add the remaining eight rows as shown in the assembly diagram.

7 Secure the seam allowances on the corners of each square using a blind appliqué stitch approximately 1" along the edge from each corner. Fold in the seam allowance ½" on the outer edges of the quilt and secure all along with a blind appliqué stitch. (Fig. 4)

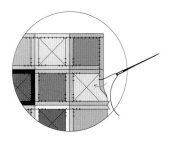

Figure 4

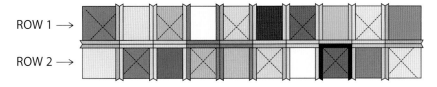

Figure 3

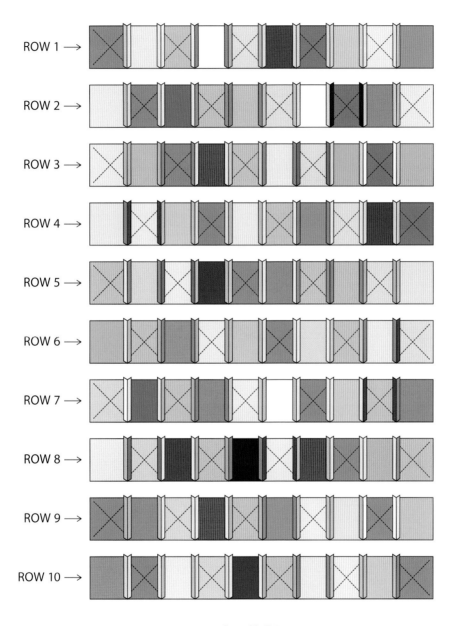

Assembly Diagram

BLOSSOM

The 1950s was an exciting decade with the launch of the Liberty Design Studio. Mid-century designers were invited to work in-house for the first time, close to bustling Carnaby Street, and to keep the company ahead of the times by responding to the world around them. Female textile designers came to the forefront and Colleen Farr set up the original team, later to be joined by her sister Gillian.

Gillian Farr designed a Liberty print we all know and love, named Mitsi. The design is made up of flowers based on the cherry blossom or Sakura, which for centuries has held a special place in Japanese culture as celebrated by Hanami (flower festivals). Liberty has always had a love of Japan and over the years has stocked many Japanese goods. Gillian embraced this heritage, but created a fresh and original print. It is beautifully simple and has been printed in many different colourways since. It has also been drawn in miniature for a version known as Mitsi Valeria. I have chosen a more recent favourite on Tana Lawn named Ffion. Like Mitsi, this is also deliberately reminiscent of cherry blossom and was inspired by a simple woodblock design created for Liberty in 1959. They all sit very harmoniously with each other, and the Spring colours remind me of blossom falling from the trees in my hometown.

The pattern for Blossom is a simple tree, which reflects the modern mid-century aesthetic Liberty has adopted. This versatile block can be stitched into a table runner, a cute pincushion or would make a pretty quilt. It is the perfect project for building your confidence in Foundation Paper Piecing.

From top: Mitsi Blue, Ffion Pink, Mitsi Red.

BLOSSOM TABLE RUNNER

Finished Quilt Size: 35" × 11" • *Finished Block Size:* 8"

MATERIALS

Mitsi Red: ¼ yard (23 cm)

Mitsi Blue: ¼ yard (23 cm)

Ffion Pink: ¼ yard (23 cm)

Ffion Yellow: ¼ yard (23 cm)

Wiltshire Shade Cream: ½ yard (46 cm)

Wiltshire Shade Blue: ¼ yard (23 cm)

Mitsi Blue: ½ yard (46 cm) for the backing

Batting: 39" × 15" (1 m × 38 cm)

Templates (see pages 204–206)

CUTTING

From the Wiltshire Shade Blue, cut:

(2) 35½" × 2" rectangles

(2) 8½" × 2" rectangles

PREPARATION

Make 4 copies of each of the templates on pages 204–206

ASSEMBLING THE RUNNER

1 Foundation Paper Piece (see page 191) four tree blocks, one of each colour. (Fig. 1)

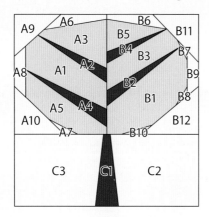

Figure 1

2 Referencing Figure 2 for colour placement, join the four Tree Blocks into a row. Remove the papers and press.

3 Join the 2" × 8½" Wiltshire Shade Blue borders to the left and right of the assembled unit from Step 2 and press towards the borders.

4 Repeat Step 3 to join the 35½" borders to the top and bottom.

QUILTING

Position and secure the tablerunner top to the batting and quilt. Blossom is quilted with straight lines running horizontally across the quilt, 1" apart.

> TIP: *The wonderful thing about Foundation Paper Piecing, is that no matter how tiny the piece, the construction remains the same. This makes working with smaller cuts of fabric much easier than if they were traditionally pieced. Try making the pincushion version of Blossom for a friend or for a swap and you will see!*

FINISHING

Trim away the excess batting. Pin the Mitsi Blue 35½" x 11½" backing rectangle to the assembled top, right sides together and align the raw edges. Using a ¼" seam

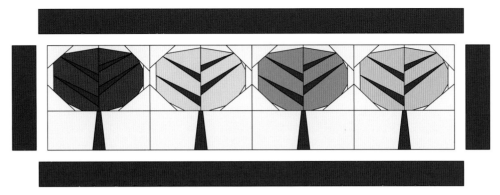

Figure 2

allowance, sew around the perimeter of the rectangle leaving a 4" gap along the bottom edge for turning. Secure your stitches at the beginning and end. Clip the corners close to the stitching to reduce the bulk, being careful not to cut through the stitches. Turn through with the right side out. Gently poke out the corners and Ladder stitch the gap closed (see page 68).

BLOSSOM PINCUSHION

Finished Size: 6" × 6" • *Finished Block Size:* 4"

MATERIALS

Mitsi Green: 7" (18 cm) square

Ffion Yellow: 7" (18 cm) square for backing

Mitsi Valeria Red: 6" (15 cm) square

Wiltshire Shade Cream: 6" (15 cm) square

Wiltshire Shade Blue: 3" (8 cm) square

Templates (see page 203)

Stuffing

Point turner

CUTTING

From the Mitsi Green, cut:
(2) 7" × 1¾" rectangles
(2) 4½" × 1¾" rectangles

PREPARATION

Make single copies of the templates on page 203

ASSEMBLING THE PINCUSHION

1 Foundation Paper Piece (see page 191) templates A, B, and C. Sew the templates together. (Fig. 1)

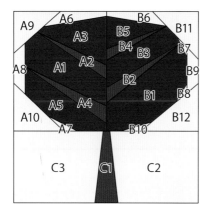

Figure 1

2 Remove the papers and press.

3 Join the 4½" borders to the left and right of the Tree Block and press towards the borders.

4 Join the 7" borders to the top and bottom.

5 Pin the Ffion Yellow 7" backing square to the assembled top from Step 4, right sides together and aligning the raw edges. Using a ½" seam allowance, sew around the perimeter of the square leaving a 1" gap along the bottom edge for turning. Secure your stitches at the beginning and end. Clip the corners close to the stitching to reduce the bulk, being careful not to cut through the stitches. (Fig. 2)

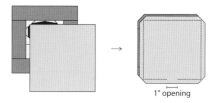

1" opening

Figure 2

6 Turn through with the right side out. Gently poke out the corners and insert the toy stuffing.

> **TIP**: *You may want to also include walnut shells, a pattern weight or shavings to add some extra stability to the pincushion.*

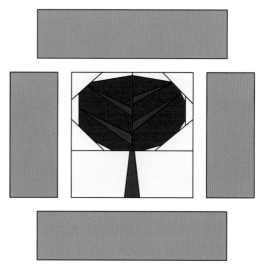

Assembly Diagram

7 Ladder stitch the gap closed (see page 68).

BERRY

The Wiltshire berry print was created for Liberty in 1933 by the same elusive designer of Betsy, who sadly, we can only identify by the initials DS. This print was revived and re-coloured by the Liberty Design Studio in 1968 and has appeared on Tana Lawn in numerous colourways since the late seventies. Most quilters I know have a soft spot for this print and have a little of it in their stash. An exciting development at Liberty Fabrics is having this iconic design reimagined into a two colour silhouette, Wiltshire Shadow, printed on Lasenby cotton. This is perfect for combining with Tana Lawn as I have done in my Berry Quilt. A recent addition is a small version of Wiltshire Berry on Tana Lawn named Wiltshire Bud which I was delighted to include.

The Orange Peel quilt block was invented many years before Liberty began making fabric. Yet, I am always struck by how contemporary it looks and I knew instantly that I could use it to echo the curves of the berry and leaf shapes on Wiltshire fabric. I was also inspired by 1960s fashion designer Mary Quant, who used Liberty fabrics, and is famous for her pop art vibe and daisy motif. This sparked the idea of a modern, offset medallion quilt design and gave me the perfect opportunity to explore curved piecing.

I'm always keen to mix fabrics and textures, so in this quilt I have used Oakshott Cottons which give a shimmer in changing light, due to the different colours of the warp and the weft. The colour palette is called Scandinavia. In my view, this really makes the different tones of the Wiltshire Tana Lawn prints sing. The dark blue is Lasenby cotton, and the Avocado Oakshott binding finishes the quilt off with a pop of colour.

The Berry Quilt encourages you to be playful with texture and colour as well as using just a small amount of Liberty Fabric prints for big impact. Why not select your favourite Wiltshire fabrics and blenders, embracing the daring spirit of the swinging sixties? I promise you that sewing curves is a lot of fun!

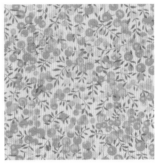

From top: Wiltshire Light Blue, Wiltshire Bud Yellow, Wiltshire Red.

BERRY

Finished Quilt Size: 90" × 95" • *Finished Block Size:* 5"

MATERIALS

Liberty Fabrics

Wiltshire Light Blue: ⅝ yard (57 cm)

Wiltshire Pink: ¼ yard (23 cm)

Wiltshire Bud Pink: ¼ yard (23 cm)

Wiltshire Bud Yellow: ¼ yard (23 cm)

Wiltshire Red: ¼ yard (23 cm)

Wiltshire Dark Blue: ½ yard (46 cm)

Wiltshire Shade Blue: ⅝ yard (57 cm)

Wiltshire Green: 5½ yards (5.03 m) for the backing

Oakshott Fabrics

Bergen Cream: 1¼ yards (1.14 m)

Oslo Lilac: 1¼ yards (1.14 m)

Uppsala Light Grey: 1 yard (91 cm)

Stockholm Dark Grey: ¾ yard (69 cm)

Malmo Blue: 1 yard (91 cm)

Copenhagen Green: 1 yard (91 cm)

Tromso Pink: 1 yard (91 cm)

Helsinki Yellow: ¾ yard (69 cm)

Avocado Green: ¾ yard (69 cm) for the binding

Batting: 98" × 107" (2.49 m × 2.72 m)

Hera Marker

Template plastic

Scissors for cutting template plastic

TEMPLATES

1 Acrylic templates for the Berry quilt are available to buy from jenni-smith.co.uk or you will need a set of 5" and 3¾" Drunkard's Path templates

2 Alternatively, copy the Berry Templates on pages 194–196 onto template plastic.

CUTTING

From the Wiltshire Light Blue, cut:

(2) 6" × 52" strips, subcut into:

  (10) 7" × 6" rectangles, subcut into:

    (2) 5" concave Berry Templates from each to make a total of 20

  (2) 10½" × 6" rectangles, subcut into:

    (2) 5" convex Berry Template from each to make a total of 4

(1) 4½" × 52" strip, subcut into:

  (5) 4½" squares, subcut into:

    (1) 3¾" convex Berry Template from each to make a total of 5

From the Wiltshire Pink, cut:

(1) 6" × 52" strip, subcut into:

  (2) 10½" × 6" rectangles, subcut into:

    (2) 5" convex Berry Template from each to make a total of 4

  (2) 6" × 7" rectangles, subut into:

    (2) 5" concave Berry Template from each to make a total of 4

  (2) 4½" × 8½" rectangles, subcut into:

    (2) 3¾" convex Berry Template from each to make a total of 4

From the Wiltshire Bud Pink, cut:

(1) 6" × 52" strip, subcut into:

  (2) 10½" × 6" rectangles, subcut into:

    (2) 5" convex Berry Template from each to make a total of 4

(1) 8½" × 4½" rectangle, subcut into:

    (2) 3¾" convex Berry Template total of 2

*From the Wiltshire Bud
Yellow, cut:*

(1) 6" × 52½" strip, subcut into:
    (5) 10½" × 6" rectangles,
    subcut into:
        (2) 5" convex Berry
        Template from each
        to make a total of 10

From the Wiltshire Red, cut:

(1) 6" × 52" strip, subcut into:
    (3) 6" × 10½" rectangles,
    subcut into:
        (2) 5" convex Berry
        Template from each
        to make a total of 6

    (3) 4½" squares, subcut
    into:
        (1) 3¾" convex Berry
        Template from each
        to make a total of 3

*From the Wiltshire Dark
Blue, cut:*

(2) 6" × 52½" strips, subcut
into:
    (9) 10½" × 6" rectangles,
    subcut into:
        (2) 5" convex Berry
        Template from each
        to make a total of 18

    (2) 4½" squares, subcut
    into:
        (1) 3¾" convex Berry
        Template from each
        to make a total of 2

*From the Wiltshire Shade
Blue, cut:*

(3) 6" × 42" strips, subcut into:
    (18) 6" × 7" rectangles,
    subcut into:
        (2) 5" concave Berry
        Template from 17

rectangles and one
from the final to make
a total of 35

*From the Oakshott Bergen
Cream cut:*

(3) 5½" × 52" strips, subcut
into:
    (27) 5½" squares

(4) 6" × 52" strips, subcut
into:
    (20) 7" × 6" rectangles,
    subcut into:
        (2) 5" concave Berry
        Template from each
        to make a total of 40

    (2) 10½" × 6" rectangles,
    subcut into:
        (2) 5" convex Berry
        Template from each to
        make a total of 4

(4) 8½" × 6" rectangles,
subcut into:
    (2) 3¾" concave Berry
    Template from each
    to make a total of 8

*From the Oakshott Oslo Lilac,
cut:*

(4) 5½" × 52" strips, subcut
into:
    (35) 5½" squares

(2) 6" × 52" strips, subcut
into:
    (4) 10½" × 6" rectangles,
    subcut into:
        (2) 5" convex Berry
        Template from three
        of the strips and one
        from the final to make
        a total of 7

(2) 7" × 6" rectangles,
subcut into:
    (2) 5" concave Berry
    Template from each
    to make a total of 4

(1) 4½" square, subcut
into:
    (1) 3¾" concave Berry
    Template

*From the Oakshott Uppsala
Light Grey, cut:*

(4) 5½" × 52" strips, subcut
into:
    (33) 5½" squares

(1) 6" × 52" strip, subcut into:
    (2) 10½" × 6" rectangles,
    subcut into:
        (2) 5" convex Berry
        Template from each
        to make a total of 4

    (1) 8½" × 6" rectangle,
    subcut into:
        (2) 3¾" concave Berry
        Template

    (1) 7" × 6" rectangle,
    subcut into:
        (2) 5" concave Berry
        Template

*From the Oakshott Stockholm
Dark Grey, cut:*

(3) 5½" × 52" strips, subcut
into:
    (24) 5½" squares

(1) 6" × 52" strip, subcut into:
    (2) 10½" × 6" rectangles,
    subcut into:
        (2) 5" convex Berry
        Template from each
        to make a total of 4

(4) 7" × 6" rectangles, subcut into:

> (2) 5" concave Berry Template from each to make a total of 8

From the Oakshott Malmo Blue, cut:

(4) 5½" × 52" strips, subcut into:

> (35) 5½" squares

(1) 6" × 52" strip, subcut into:

> (3) 5" convex Berry Template

> (1) 3¾" concave Berry Template

From the Oakshott Copenhagen Green, cut:

(4) 5½" × 52" strips, subcut into:

> (32) 5½" squares

(1) 6" × 52" strip, subcut into:

> (2) 10½" × 6" rectangles, subcut into:

(2) 5" convex Berry Template from each to make a total of 4

(1) 7" × 6" rectangle, subcut into:

> (2) 5" concave Berry Template

> (1) 4½" square, subcut into:

> > (1) 3¾" concave Berry Template

From the Oakshott Tromso Pink, cut:

(4) 5½" × 52" strips, subcut into:

> (31) 5½" squares

(1) 6" × 52" strip, subcut into:

> (2) 10½" × 6" rectangles, subcut into:

> > (2) 5" convex Berry Template from one rectangle and (1) from the second rectangle for a total of 3

(1) 8½" × 6" rectangle, subcut into:

> (2) 3¾" concave Berry Template

(2) 7" × 6" rectangles, subcut into:

> (2) 5" concave Berry Template from each to make a total of 4

From the Oakshott Helsinki Yellow, cut:

(3) 5½" × 52" strips, subcut into:

> (27) 5½" squares

(1) 6" × 52" strip, subcut into:

> (5) 5½" squares, (2) 5" convex Berry Template and (1) 3¾" concave Berry Template

From the Oakshott Avocado Green, cut:

(8) 2½" × 52" strips for the binding

GENERAL DRUNKARD'S PATH BLOCK ASSEMBLY

1 Position one concave piece on top of a corresponding convex piece of the same size. Ensure that the right sides of the fabric are facing and that the raw edges align at the corners.

2 Sew in a straight line for the first ½" before beginning to match the curve of the raw edges. To do this, gently ease in the excess fabric, taking care not to stretch the top piece but still ensuring the raw edges of the curve align. (Fig. 1)

> **TIP:** *It is personal preference whether to pin the layers together before sewing but I recommend sewing without pins. The block will be trimmed at the end, so don't panic if your ends don't seem to match perfectly at first. I recommend easing the curve as you sew, ensuring the raw edges align as you progress. While it can seem daunting at first, practice on a few spare pieces of fabric to gain mastery.*

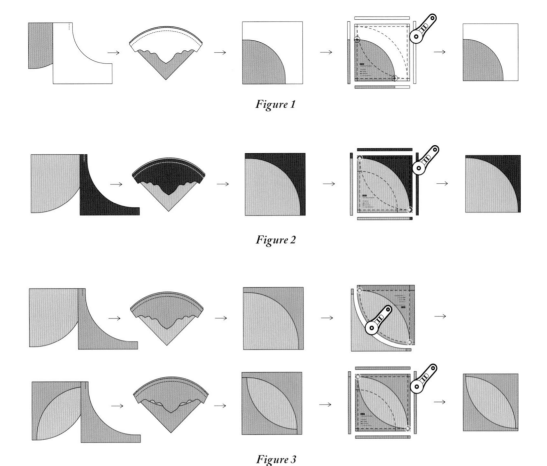

Figure 1

Figure 2

Figure 3

3 Continue sewing to the end of the curve, matching the corners again at the end.

4 Press the seam open.

5 Referencing Figures 1 or 2, trim the block to size using the Trimming Template (page 196). Align the seams of the curve with the dashed template markings. Pay close attention to the highlighted circles, making sure they sit where the seams meet. Then trim away the excess background fabric to 5½" square.

ASSEMBLING THE ORANGE PEEL BLOCK

1 Position a 5" concave piece on top of a corresponding 5" convex piece. Ensure that the right sides of the fabric are facing and that the raw edges at the corners align.

2 Sew in a straight line for the first ½" before beginning to match the curved edges.

3 Match the outside edges by gently easing in the excess fabric, taking care not to stretch the top piece.

4 Continue sewing to the end of the curve, matching the corners at the end.

5 Press the seams open.

6 Trim the block using the 5" Convex template as shown in Figure 3.

7 Position another 5" convex piece on top of the unit created in step 6 RST.

8 Repeat steps 2–4.

9 Referencing Figure 3, trim the block using the Trimming Template. The block will measure 5½" square.

ASSEMBLING THE CENTRAL MEDALLION

1 Create (12) 5½" Drunkards Path Blocks using the 5" concave Wiltshire Shade Blue and the 5" convex Wiltshire Dark Blue pieces. (Fig. 4)

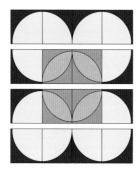

Figure 4

2 Create (4) 5½" Orange Peel Blocks using the 5" convex Oakshott Oslo Lilac and the 5" concave Wiltshire Light Blue.

3 Referencing Figure 4, arrange the trimmed blocks into a grid of four rows

of four blocks each. Double check that the orientation of the blocks is correct before sewing them into rows.

4 Press the seams for each row in opposite directions.

5 Join the four rows together, nesting the seams and pressing them downward.

ASSEMBLING THE VINES

1 Set aside four of the 5" Wiltshire Bud Yellow convex shapes. Using the (30) remaining 5" convex shapes from the assorted Liberty prints and 60 Oakshott 5" concave shapes, create (30) 5½" trimmed Orange Peel Blocks.

2 Pair like-coloured Liberty Orange Peel blocks into 2 columns of 2 or 3 rows to create vine blocks. Refer to the assembly diagram for pairings. (Fig. 5)

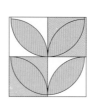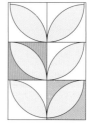

Figure 5

3 Join blocks into rows, pressing the seams for each row in opposite directions.

4 Join the rows together, nesting the seams and pressing them downward. Repeat to make (3) 10½" square vine blocks and (3) more, measuring 10½" × 15½". (Fig. 5)

ASSEMBLING THE CIRCLE BLOCKS

1 Using the (16) 3¾" convex shapes from the assorted Liberty prints and the (16) 3¾" concave Oakshott shapes, create (16) 5½" trimmed Drunkards Path Blocks.

2 Randomly pair (4) 5½" trimmed Drunkards Path Blocks into (4) circle blocks or refer to the assembly diagram for the exact pairings. (Fig. 6)

Figure 6

3 Join blocks into rows, pressing the seams for each row in opposite directions.

4 Join the rows together, nesting the seams and pressing them downward. Repeat to make (4) 10½" square circle blocks. (Fig. 6)

ASSEMBLING THE STAR BLOCKS

1 Create (8) 5½" trimmed Orange Peel Blocks using the (4) 5" Wiltshire Bud Yellow convex shapes and (4) 5" Oakshott cream convex shapes, paired with (16) 5" concave shapes from the assorted Liberty prints.

2 Randomly pair (4) 5½" trimmed Orange Peel Blocks into (2) star blocks or refer to the assembly diagram for the exact pairings that were used. (Fig. 7)

Figure 7

3 Join blocks into rows, pressing the seams for each row in opposite directions.

4 Join the rows together, nesting the seams and pressing them downward. Repeat to make (2) 10½" square star blocks. (Fig. 7)

ASSEMBLING THE BURST BLOCKS

From the remaining cut curved units, create (23) 5½" Drunkards Path blocks. (Fig. 8)

Figure 8

ASSEMBLING THE SECTIONS
SECTIONS 1, 2, 3, 4

1 Referencing the Assembly Diagram for placement, lay out each section into a grid of 10 rows of 4 blocks each. Intermix a variety of 5½" Oakshott solid squares to fill in the rest of the grid.

2 Referencing the Assembly Diagram, sew the blocks together into rows. Press the seams for each row in opposite directions. Join the rows and alternate pressing seams upward and downward for each section.

SECTION 5

1 Referencing the Assembly Diagram for placement, lay out the section into a grid of 10 rows of 2 blocks each. Intermix a variety of 5½" Oakshott solid squares to fill in the rest of the grid.

2 Referencing the Assembly Diagram, sew blocks together into rows. Press the seams for each row in opposite directions. Join the rows and press the seams in the opposite direction used to that used in Section 4.

SECTIONS 6, 7, 8, 9

1 Referencing the Assembly Diagram for placement, lay out each section into a grid of 9 rows of 4 blocks each. Intermix a variety of 5½" Oakshott solid squares to fill in the rest of the grid.

2 Referencing the Assembly Diagram, sew blocks together into rows. Press the seams for each row in opposite directions. Join the rows and alternate pressing the seams upward and downward for each section.

Archive Wiltshire swatches. These can be used as a starting point to create a fresh palette for a Berry quilt.

SECTION 10

1 Referencing the Assembly Diagram for placement, lay out the section into a grid of 9 rows of 2 blocks each. Intermix a variety of 5½" Oakshott solid squares to fill in the rest of the grid.

2 Referencing the Assembly Diagram, sew the blocks together into rows. Press the seams for each row in opposite directions. Join the rows. Press the seams in the opposite direction to that used in Section 9.

ASSEMBLING THE QUILT TOP

1 Referencing the Assembly Diagram, nest the seams and sew Sections 1, 2, 3, 4, and 5 together into one long row. Press the seams in one direction.

2 Referencing the Assembly Diagram, nest the seams and sew Sections 6, 7, 8, 9, and 10 together into one long row. Press the seams in the opposite direction used in Step 1.

3 Join the top and bottom of the quilt, nesting the seams between sewn sections. Press the seam down.

4 Press the entire top well.

QUILTING

The Berry quilt has been quilted in the ditch along all vertical and horizontal seams. There are also Orange Peel shapes quilted into some of the solid squares, using various colours from the quilt, to echo the shapes in the design. To do this, use the 5" Convex Template and Hera marker to score a line as a guide.

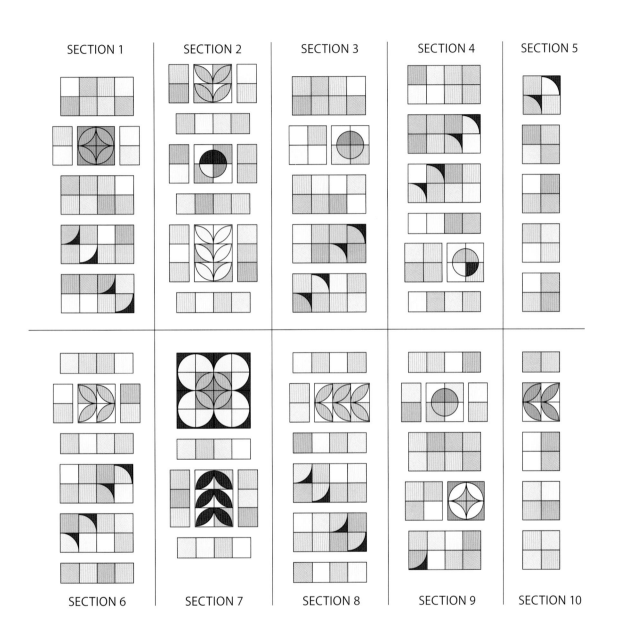

SECTION 1   SECTION 2   SECTION 3   SECTION 4   SECTION 5

SECTION 6   SECTION 7   SECTION 8   SECTION 9   SECTION 10

Assembly Diagram

ZIGZAG

The adjective "classic" describes something judged over a period of time to be outstanding and of established value. The Liberty Classics collection was formed in 1979 and these collections, updated annually, are often where we find our favourite Tana Lawn prints. These are patterns that as makers, we know and trust. Their names are engraved in our memory like old friends. Classics are re-printed as opposed to Limited Editions and will often be re-imagined in new colourways by the Design Studio.

The Zigzag Quilt was designed to incorporate Liberty prints from the seventies and those included in the first Liberty Classics collection in 1979. All of them are still available in the recent Classics and have most certainly stood the test of time.

Capel is a one-colour floral — simple and versatile, which was first printed in 1978. Pepper was designed for Liberty by the Jack Prince Studio in 1974 and is equally brilliant for many projects, blending well with other prints. Emma and Georgina is a merging of a tiny dense floral print from the 1970s called Emmy and the print Georgina. The print Thorpe was drawn in 1968 but was brought back for The Classics launch eleven years later.

The seventies also saw a flourish of majestic paisleys on Liberty prints, successfully showcased in fashion garments and interiors, but equally stunning in quilts. I used the beautiful Lee Manor paisley Tana Lawn on the back of the quilt and love how the swirling motifs contrast with the vertical piecing on the quilt top.

From top: Thorpe, Capel, Mike.

The Zigzag design alludes to the Minimalist Movement in popular culture, again from the 1970s. The simple forms and lines inspired a later Liberty print called Mike, which provides a perfect layout for a modern heirloom.

ZIGZAG

Finished Quilt Size: 52" × 80" • *Finished Column Size:* 2"

MATERIALS

Capel Indigo: 1 yard
(91 cm)

Pepper Blue: ⅜ yard
(34 cm)

Capel Pale Blue: 1 yard
(91 cm)

Capel Grey: 1 yard (91 cm)

Thorpe Blue: ¾ yard (69 cm)

Emma & Georgina Blue: ½
yard (46 cm)

Capel Indigo: ½ yard
(46 cm) for the binding

Lee Manor Blue: 3⅜ yards
(3.09 m) for the backing

Batting: 58" × 88"
(1.47 m × 2.24 m)

Acrylic ruler with a
45-degree marking

Fine chalk pencil

CUTTING

TIP: *Gentle pressing and
accurate cutting are essential for
this quilt. If possible, use a 24"
ruler and a large cutting mat to
minimize the number of times
you need to fold the yardage
before cutting the long strips*

From the Capel Indigo (A), cut:
(13) 2½" × 52" strips, subcut
into:

(4) 2½" × 33" rectangles

(6) 2½" × 30" rectangles

(1) 2½" × 28" rectangle

(4) 2½" × 22½" rectangles

(3) 2½" × 20½" rectangles

(3) 2½" × 15½" rectangles

(2) 2½" × 13" rectangles

(3) 2½" × 10½" rectangles

(2) 2½" × 8" rectangles

(2) 2½" × 5½" rectangles

From the Pepper Blue (B), cut:
(4) 2½" × 52" strips, subcut
into:

(1) 2½" × 28" rectangle

(2) 2½" × 27½" rectangles

(1) 2½" × 22½" rectangle

(1) 2½" × 20" rectangle

(1) 2½" × 17½" rectangle

(1) 2½" × 15½" rectangle

(1) 2½" × 10½" rectangle

(1) 2½" × 8" rectangle

*From the Capel Pale Blue (C),
cut:*
(10) 2½" × 52" strips, subcut
into:

(1) 2½" × 32½" rectangle

(1) 2½" × 30" rectangle

(1) 2½" × 27½" rectangle

(4) 2½" × 23" rectangles

(1) 2½" × 20½" rectangle

(3) 2½" × 20" rectangles

(1) 2½" × 19½" rectangle

(7) 2½" × 17½" rectangles

(2) 2½" × 15½" rectangles

(4) 2½" × 8" rectangles

(1) 2½" × 5½" rectangle

From the Capel Grey (D), cut:
(11) 2½" × 52" strips, subcut
into:

(1) 2½" × 33" rectangle

(4) 2½" × 30" rectangles

(3) 2½" × 28" rectangles

(3) 2½" × 27½" rectangles

(1) 2½" × 22½" rectangle

(3) 2½" × 20½" rectangles

(2) 2½" × 20" rectangles

(2) 2½" × 17½" rectangles

(1) 2½" × 15½" rectangle

(1) 2½" × 10½" rectangle

From the Thorpe Blue (E), cut:
(9) 2½" × 52" strips, subcut
into:

(2) 2½" × 30" rectangles

(1) 2½" × 28" rectangle

(3) 2½" × 27½" rectangles

(2) 2½" × 22½" rectangles

(1) 2½" × 20½" rectangle

(2) 2½" × 20" rectangles

(6) 2½" × 17½" rectangles

(1) 2½" × 10½" rectangle

(2) 2½" × 5½" rectangles

From the Emma & Georgina Blue (F), cut:
(4) 2½" × 52" strips, subcut into:
   (1) 2½" × 32½" rectangle

(2) 2½" × 30" rectangles
(1) 2½" × 23" rectangle
(1) 2½" × 20½" rectangle
(1) 2½" × 5½" rectangle

From the Capel Indigo, cut:
(6) 2½" × 52" strips for the binding

ASSEMBLING THE COLUMNS

1 Referencing the Piecing Diagram (see page 134), arrange the cut strips vertically.

2 Position the two rectangles in Column 1 right sides together. Align the bottom of the 13" rectangle with the top of the 22½" rectangle at a right angle (just like making bias binding strips!). Using a fine chalk pencil, draw a diagonal line on the wrong side of the 22½" rectangle using the 45-degree marking on an acrylic ruler. Pin and sew on the drawn line.

3 Trim away the outer corner, ¼" away from the sewn line in Step 2 and press the seam towards the 22½" rectangle. (Fig. 1)

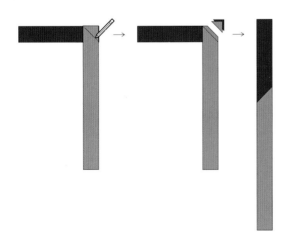

Figure 1

4 Repeat Steps 2–3 to attach all of the rectangles in each column. Be sure to number each column with a temporary label to prevent confusion!

ASSEMBLING THE QUILT TOP

1 Attach the first five assembled Columns together, beginning with Column 1 and working from left to right. Alternate by stitching from top to bottom, then bottom to top each time you add a new strip to prevent twisting. Press all of the seams in the same direction before attaching the next strip. Be sure to press first on the wrong side of the fabric, then the right side, to ensure that strips lay flat (see page 135).

> **TIP**: *Even though you may not be a fan of pins, because these are such long strips, I recommend using them at regular intervals along the length for this project. They really will make a big difference!*

2 Continue sewing columns together in groups of 4, 4, 4, 4, and 5.

3 Join the first three vertical sections together to form one half of the top. Repeat for the last three vertical sections.

4 Join the two halves from Step 3 and press.

1
A 2½" × 13"
B 2½" × 22½"
C 2½" × 32½"
A 2½" × 20½"
2
D 2½" × 20½"
A 2½" × 22½"
C 2½" × 17½"
D 2½" × 28"
3
C 2½" × 8"
E 2½" × 17½"
C 2½" × 20"
A 2½" × 30"
B 2½" × 15½"
4
F 2½" × 5½"
D 2½" × 27½"
F 2½" × 30"
D 2½" × 17½"
B 2½" × 10½"
5
A 2½" × 8"
B 2½" × 20"
C 2½" × 20"
E 2½" × 27½"
A 2½" × 15½"
6
A 2½" × 33"
D 2½" × 30"
C 2½" × 23"
7
C 2½" × 5½"
D 2½" × 27½"
A 2½" × 30"
B 2½" × 17½"
A 2½" × 10½"
8
C 2½" × 8"
E 2½" × 17½"
C 2½" × 20"
A 2½" × 30"
D 2½" × 15½"
9
A 2½" × 33"
D 2½" × 30"
C 2½" × 23"
10
D 2½" × 20½"
A 2½" × 22½"
C 2½" × 17½"
E 2½" × 28"
11
A 2½" × 13"
E 2½" × 22½"
F 2½" × 32½"
A 2½" × 20½"
12
E 2½" × 5½"
C 2½" × 27½"
D 2½" × 30"
C 2½" × 17½"
E 2½" × 10½"
13
A 2½" × 5½"
B 2½" × 27½"
A 2½" × 30"
E 2½" × 17½"
A 2½" × 10½"
14
A 2½" × 20½"
D 2½" × 22½"
C 2½" × 17½"
D 2½" × 28"
15
B 2½" × 8"
C 2½" × 17½"
E 2½" × 20"
A 2½" × 30"
C 2½" × 15½"
16
A 2½" × 33"
E 2½" × 30"
C 2½" × 23"
17
C 2½" × 8"
F 2½" × 20½"
C 2½" × 19½"
E 2½" × 27½"
A 2½" × 15½"
18
E 2½" × 20½"
A 2½" × 22½"
C 2½" × 17½"
D 2½" × 28"
19
D 2½" × 33"
E 2½" × 30"
C 2½" × 23"
20
C 2½" × 20½"
A 2½" × 22½"
D 2½" × 17½"
A 2½" × 28"
21
E 2½" × 5½"
B 2½" × 27½"
F 2½" × 30"
E 2½" × 17½"
D 2½" × 10½"
22
A 2½" × 5½"
D 2½" × 27½"
C 2½" × 30"
E 2½" × 17½"
A 2½" × 10½"
23
C 2½" × 8"
E 2½" × 17½"
D 2½" × 20"
A 2½" × 30"
C 2½" × 15½"
24
A 2½" × 33"
D 2½" × 30"
F 2½" × 23"
25
D 2½" × 20½"
E 2½" × 22½"
C 2½" × 17½"
B 2½" × 28"
26
A 2½" × 8"
E 2½" × 20"
D 2½" × 20"
E 2½" × 27½"
A 2½" × 15½"

Piecing Diagram

QUILT

Zig Zag has been quilted with lines 2" apart on a 45-degree angle to mirror the joins in the strips.

Assembly Diagram

GEO

I was first introduced to Liberty Fabrics in the 1980s as I lived close to one of the mills in Lancashire where they printed cotton. (The Merton print works having closed in 1972). As a child I had a lazy left eye and had to go for hospital appointments not far from the Liberty shop which was attached to the mill. My post-appointment treat was an occasional fabric shopping spree and I was instantly drawn to the soft touch of the Tana Lawn, so my Nanny Gladys bought me a little bit and the rest is history!

The 1980s saw a revival of Liberty florals. I think it is testament to the quality of Liberty designs that they can be nostalgic for the English country cottage look from this decade, and yet remain timeless.

I designed the Geo Quilt by imagining what I would have loved in the bedroom of my childhood dreams. It has a very pretty combination of Liberty fabrics from the period including Sarah, Rachel and Swirling Petals which I have mixed up with florals from more recent decades. This project lends itself to using your stash, and I had fun playing with different scale of prints to keep the eye moving. In fact, I got totally carried away with how beautiful they all are and in total I included 33 individual designs on Tana Lawn. However you could be more restrained than me!

The large geometric quilt blocks remind me of Aztec style designs. These were printed on garments and album covers in my youth, during the 1980s, as well as Liberty fabrics designed by the Cloth Collective and the exceptional duo Collier-Campbell.

The solid background fabric is also Tana Lawn, making this large quilt feel luxuriously soft and lightweight. The close weave of the fabric is brilliant when cutting on the bias, as it does not stretch and makes working with triangles and matching points a breeze! Indulging yourself with this substrate on the back of a quilt also means you can go to sleep snuggled beneath silk-like cotton.

From top: Poppy & Daisy, Margaret Annie, Felicite.

GEO

Finished Quilt Size: 82" × 90" • *Finished Block Size:* 6"

MATERIALS

Tana Lawn Cream:
3¾ yards (3.43 m)

Margaret Annie Blue:
1 yard (91 cm)

¼ yard (23 cm) each of *Poppy & Daisy M, Eloise B, Betsy Ann Red, Rachel D, Phoebe Pink, Thorpe Hill Pink, Betsy Ann Pink, Michelle A, Donna Leigh Green, Swirling Petals Red, Felicite Yellow, Elysian Day Red, D'Anjo Pink, Libby C, Poppy Forest Pink, Clementina D, Margaret Annie A, Wiltshire Bud Pink, Annabella A, Felicite Blue, Danuna Green, Ciara A,*

Elysian Day Yellow, Mauvey Blue, Mauvey Pink, Tresco A-CC, Tatum K, D'Anjo Blue, Danuna Blue, Glenjade Blue

Sarah F: ¾ yard (69 cm) for the binding

Glenjade Grey: 5⅜ yards (4.91 m) for the backing

Batting: 96" × 98" (2.44 m × 2.49m)

CUTTING

From the Tana Cream, cut:
(8) 6⅞" × 52" strips, subcut into:

    (50) 6⅞" squares

    (18) 6½" × 2½" rectangles

(6) 3½" × 52" strips, subcut into:

    (80) 3½" squares

    (2) 6½" × 2½" rectangles

(11) 2" × 48½" strips

(11) 2" × 36½" strips

From the Margaret Annie Blue, cut:
(8) 3½" × 52" strips

From the Sarah F, cut:
(8) 2½" × 52" strips for the binding

Cutting Instructions for the remaining fabrics:
Details are shown on the facing page

NOTE: *Geo is made using two-at-a-time HSTs. This means some of the fabrics will not maintain the same directionality, but this is absolutely fine.*

ASSEMBLING THE BLOCKS

TIP: *When piecing a project like this, I recommend using a thread colour that blends well with fabrics that are multi-coloured. Light grey or pale sage green thread disappears considerably more than white.*

ASSEMBLING THE HALF SQUARE TRIANGLE BLOCKS

1 Position (1) 6⅞" square and a background square right sides together, aligning the raw edges. Using a fine chalk pencil, draw a diagonal line on the wrong side of the background square (Figure 1).

2 Sew a ¼" seam on either side of the drawn line from Step 1, creating 2 seams. Cut along

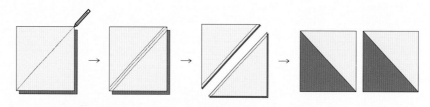

Figure 1

From the remaining fabric, cut:

FABRIC	6⅞" SQUARE(S) FOR HALF-SQUARE TRIANGLES (HSTS)	6½" x 3½" RECTANGLE(S) FOR FLYING GEESE	2½" x 6½" RECTANGLE(S) FOR RAIL FENCE
Poppy & Daisy M	2	2	1
Eloise B	2	2	0
Betsy Ann Red	2	1	1
Rachel D	1	2	2
Phoebe Pink	1	1	2
Thorpe Hill Pink	2	1	1
Betsy Ann Pink	2	1	1
Michelle A	2	2	1
Donna Leigh Green	1	3	2
Swirling Petals Red	1	2	2
Felicite Yellow	2	1	1
Elysian Day Red	1	2	1
D'Anjo Pink	2	1	1
Libby C	2	2	1
Poppy Forest Pink	1	1	2
Clementina D	2	2	1
Margaret Annie A	2	2	1
Wiltshire Bud Pink	2	1	1
Annabella A	2	1	2
Felicite Blue	2	2	1
Danuna Green	1	1	2
Ciara A	2	0	1
Elysian Day Yellow	1	1	2
Mauvey Blue	2	0	1
Mauvey Pink	2	1	2
Tresco A-CC	2	0	1
Tatum K	2	1	1
D'Anjo Blue	2	0	2
Danuna Blue	1	2	1
Glenjade Blue	1	2	2
TOTAL	**50**	**40**	**40**

the drawn line. Press towards the pattern fabric and trim away the dog ears. Each pair of 6⅞" squares will yield (2) 6½" HSTs.

3 Repeat Steps 1–2 to create all the HSTs using the Cutting Chart on page 141.

ASSEMBLING THE FLYING GEESE BLOCKS

1 Position (1) 3½" background square on a corner of a 6½" × 3½" print rectangle, aligning two of the raw edges. Draw a diagonal line on the wrong side of the background square. (Fig. 2)

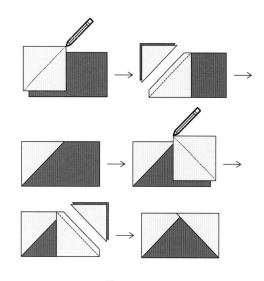

Figure 2

2 Sew along the drawn line. Trim away the outer corner ¼" away from the sewn line and press towards the Tana Lawn Pattern.

3 Position a second 3½" background square on the opposite side of the print rectangle and repeat Step 2.

4 Repeat Steps 1–3 to create (40) 6½" × 3½" Flying Geese units using the Cutting Chart on page 141.

ASSEMBLING THE RAIL FENCE BLOCK

1 Aligning the raw edges, position (1) 2½" × 6½" print rectangle and (1) 2½" × 6½" background rectangle right sides together. Pin and sew along the 6½" edge. Press towards the print.

2 Position a second 2½" × 6½" print rectangle with the unit created in Step 1. Ensure the background rectangle is positioned in the middle of the unit. Pin and sew. Press towards the print. (Fig. 3)

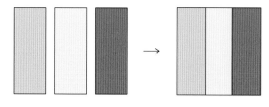

Figure 3

3 Repeat Steps 1–2 to create the remaining (19) 6½" square Rail Fence Blocks using the Cutting Chart for reference.

ASSEMBLING THE QUILT TOP

1 Referencing Figure 4, arrange the top of the quilt top on a design wall or other flat surface. Join together all of the Flying Geese units in pairs along their long edge for a total of 20 assembled units. Join together the HSTs into 10 columns of 4.

2 Repeat Step 1 for the bottom of the quilt top with all of the HST and Rail Fence units, paying carful attention to the orientation. (Fig. 5)

3 Beginning and ending with a 2" × 36½" background strip, arrange the upper 10 Columns, positioning a long background

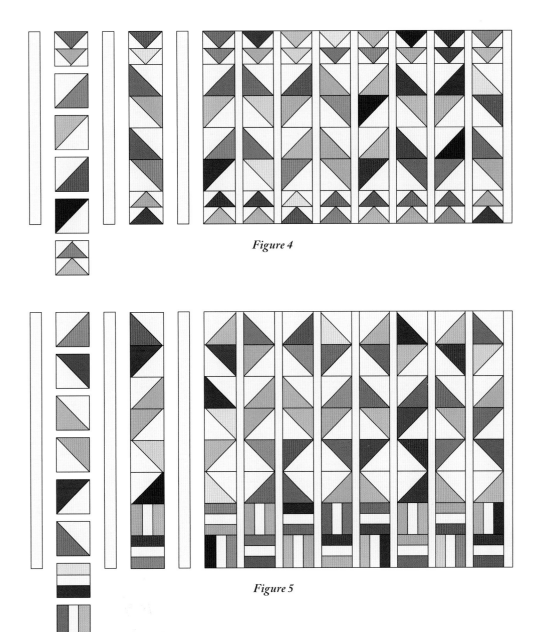

Figure 4

Figure 5

strip in between each Column. Pin and sew the columns together. Press towards the background strips.

4 Beginning and ending with a 2" × 48½" background strip, arrange the lower 10 Columns, positioning a long background

strip in between each Column. Pin and sew the Columns together. Press towards the blocks.

5 Sew the upper section to the lower section, nesting the seams. Press the seam downwards.

6 Join (2) 3½" × 52" or (3) 3½" × 42" Margaret Annie Blue Strips together using a diagonal seam (see page 188). Trim to 84½". Repeat to make another 84½" Border Strip and (2) 88½" Border Strips.

7 Join the longer borders to the left and right of the assembled unit from Step 4 and press the seams towards the borders. Add the top and bottom borders, again pressing the seams toward the borders.

QUILT

Geo has been quilted on a domestic machine using straight-line quilting to echo the shapes.

Assembly Diagram

LOVE
and
KISSES

Nothing is more exciting to me than investigating the stories behind a Liberty Print. Every single design has one — sometimes alluded to by its name, but not always. Several times per year from the late 1990s, the Liberty Design Studio explored beyond the archive, and began to release collections of prints grouped into design stories. During this dynamic period, in-house designers were given challenging, experimental briefs. They were taken on field trips to the icebergs of Reykjavik, Trecso in the Scilly Isles and Vienna, to name but a few. Sketches drawn were then worked into vibrant designs and often picked up by leading fashion designers for their collections.

Early in the millennium, Liberty also initiated incredible collaborations to design fabric prints. Artists, musicians and writers such as Grayson Perry, Edwyn Collins and Lauren Child attracted a new audience to their fabrics. Match this with the evolution of digital printing, and the creative possibilities are endless.

Love and Kisses was designed to work in a medley of prints and to showcase the cutting-edge design stories Liberty have produced since the nineties. I also wanted one project in the book to be made up of a single, repeated block so that it would be suited perfectly to a community quilt.

Sixty different people from the UK, Australia and the US, each made a block for my quilt. Everyone told their own Liberty story with the prints they selected. The finished quilt is bursting with snippets from the Liberty Fabric heritage and has an eccentric vibe that I love. In a world where few people write letters anymore, receiving a heart and a kiss in my post-box most days was also a warm and happy start to those mornings. This quilt design lends itself to spreading love for special occasions such as births, weddings and other significant milestones.

The background fabric used for each block is Wiltshire Shade Cream. I chose this because it blends so well with many Liberty prints. It also gives structure when combined with Tana Lawn, making the block a little easier to piece for people of all sewing abilities. My final recommendation is for you to ensure there is enough contrast between the fabrics for the heart and kiss.

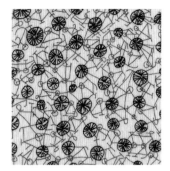

From top: Philippa, Small Susanna, Little Love.

LOVE AND KISSES

Finished Quilt Size: 72" square • *Finished Block Size:* 8"

MATERIALS

Each block in this quilt is made with various small cuts of Liberty Fabric (both Tana Lawn and Lasenby). Select your desired prints and calculate the fabric requirements based on the following:

Each traditionally pieced block will need:
(1) 5" square for the Heart
(1) 15" × 7" rectangle for the Kiss
(1) 6" background square

For one Foundation Paper-Pieced block, approximately:
(1) 8" × 12" rectangle of Kiss fabric

(1) 6" square of Heart fabric
(1) 4" × 16" background rectangle

For the whole quilt:
Wiltshire Shade Cream: 2⅛ yards (1.94 m) for the background

Oxford Fern Pink: 4½ yards (4.11 m) for the backing

Little Love Pink: ½ yard (46 cm) for the binding

Batting: 80" × 80" (2.03 m × 2.03 m)

Fine Chalk Pencil

Templates (see pages 213–214)

CUTTING (TRADITIONAL PIECING)

From the background, cut:
(24) 2⅞" × 42" strips, subcut into:
    (324) 2⅞" squares
(each block requires (4) 2⅞" squares)

For each Block:
From the Heart Fabric, cut:
(2) 2½" × 4½" rectangles

From the Kiss Fabric, cut:
(6) 2½" squares
(4) 2⅞" squares
(4) 1½" squares

From the Little Love Pink, cut:
(6) 2½" × 52" strips for the binding

TRADITIONALLY PIECING THE LOVE AND KISSES BLOCK

1 Using the 2⅞" background and Kiss Fabric squares, follow the half-square triangle block assembly instructions on pages 140–142 to create a total of 8 HSTs. Trim each of the units to 2½" square. (Fig. 1)

TIP: *There are many seams in this block, so careful pressing will help make joining and matching seams more accurate. Always press from the front and back of each unit.*

2 Position a 2½" Kiss square on the bottom of a 2½" × 4½" Heart Fabric rectangle with

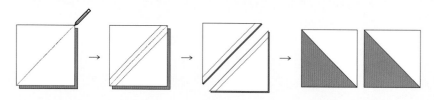

Figure 1

the right sides together. Referencing Figure 2 for placement and using a fine chalk pencil, draw a diagonal line on the wrong side of the Kiss square. Sew along the drawn line. Trim away the outer corner ¼" away from the sewn line, and press towards the Kiss fabric.

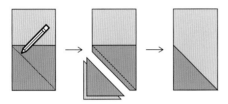

Figure 2

3 Repeat Step 2 with a second 1½" Kiss square on the top right corner of the unit created in Step 2, and again with a third 1½" Kiss square at the top left corner. (Fig. 3)

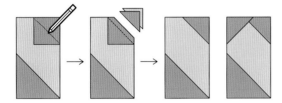

Figure 3

4 To make the opposite side of the heart, repeat Step 2, referencing Figure 4 for the directionality of the drawn line.

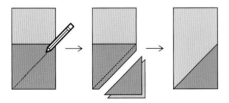

Figure 4

5 Repeat Step 3 by adding two more, to complete the right heart unit. (Fig. 5)

Figure 5

6 Referencing Figure 6, piece together in rows. Press rows 1 & 3 towards the outer Kiss squares. Press row 2 towards the central heart. Nest the seams when joining the rows.

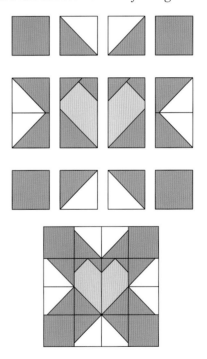

Figure 6

7 Repeat Steps 1–6 to create a total of 81 Love and Kisses blocks.

8 Alternatively, Foundation Paper Piece (FPP, ref page 191) the blocks referencing the template and assembly diagram on pages 213–214 and photocopying them 81 times. Joining the sections together as follows: A + B + D + C.

ASSEMBLING THE QUILT TOP

1 On a design wall or large surface, arrange the blocks into 9 rows of 9 blocks each. There is no fixed position for each block, so look at colour and pattern to achieve a design you are happy with.

2 Pin and sew together the first row and press the seams to the left.

3 Repeat Step 2 for the remaining rows, pressing the seams in alternate directions for each row.

4 Sew the rows together, pressing all the seams downwards.

QUILT

The Love and Kisses quilt has been quilted on the diagonal in both directions on a domestic machine. These lines create a V shape underneath the heart in the block.

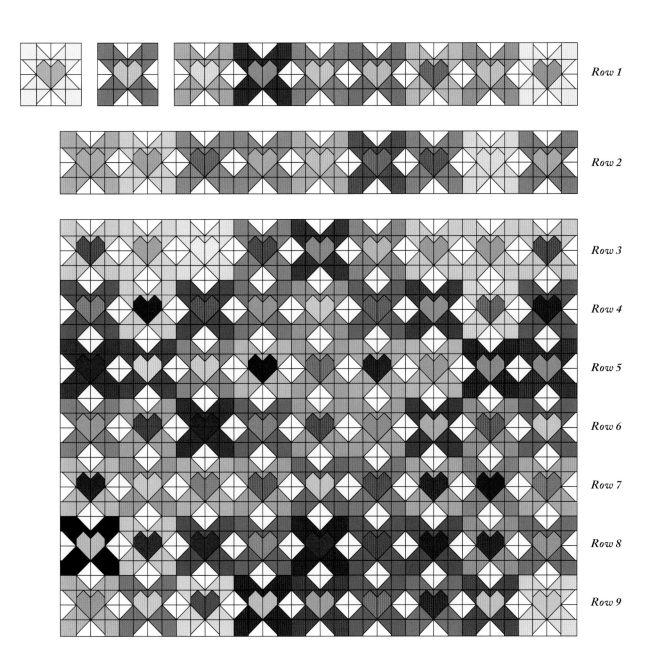

Row 1

Row 2

Row 3

Row 4

Row 5

Row 6

Row 7

Row 8

Row 9

Assembly Diagram

In the Liberty flagship interior, you can search for carvings of animals — many of which can be found in the central atrium on the third floor. This is another eccentric quirk that I love when I visit the store. There is a lion, a frog on the stairs, a monkey, an elephant, a bear and my personal favourite, the owl. They were made in a London workshop which produced Liberty Arts and Crafts furniture, as were the intricately carved panels and pillars throughout the store.

Generations of staff at Liberty have passed on the tale of how these animals come to life at night every Yuletide, causing mischief while spreading festive cheer. The creatures and their stories have inspired the design team for a number of conversational prints, including Arthur's Ark and Liberty Christmas.

Oscar Owl is a Foundation Paper Pieced project that can be used as a cushion, wall-hanging or could be repeated in a quilt. Sewing through papers on the machine, stabilises the fabric. So it is perfectly fine to combine different substrates and I have used both Tana Lawn and Lasenby Cottons. Oscar's face is made from a selection of two-colour prints, making each detail stand out. Adelajda on Tana Lawn is a dynamic star design which represents the sky. Feather Dance from the Summer House Quilting collection alludes to the feather body of a bird dressed in his Liberty shirt and scarf. Arthur's Ark was the obvious choice for the border, and comes in other pretty colourways.

From top: Liberty Christmas, Feather Dance, Arthur's Ark.

I love making projects for children with Liberty fabrics. It is playful, bright and they always enjoy searching for hidden details in each of the prints.

I named the owl after the late poet and playwright Oscar Wilde who loved Liberty and famously declared that it was "The chosen resort of the artistic shopper". A fact which is certainly still true today!

OSCAR OWL

Finished Pillow Size: 22" square • *Finished Block Size:* 12" square

MATERIALS

Wiltshire Shade Blue:
6" × 14½" (15 cm × 37 cm) rectangle for the border

Arthur's Ark Light Blue :
20" × 23½" (51 cm × 60 cm) rectangle for the border

A Fat Eighth each of *Wiltshire Shadow Silver Metallic, Cambridge Fern Blue, Cumbrian Vine Blue, Cumbrian Vine Orange, Feather Dance Orange, Feather Dance Blue*

A Fat Quarter of *Adelajda Cream*

Scraps of *Wiltshire Shadow Clementine and Blue:* For pupils and beak

Backing Fabric: (2) 22½" × 18½" (57 cm × 47 cm) rectangles

Batting: 24" × 24" (61 cm × 61 cm)

24" (60 cm) square pillow form

Templates (see pages 218–221)

CUTTING

From the Wiltshire Shade Blue, cut:
(2) 1½" × 14½" rectangles
(2) 1½" × 12½" rectangles

From the Arthur's Ark Light Blue, cut:
(2) 5" × 23½" rectangles
(2) 5" × 14½" rectangles

ASSEMBLING THE OSCAR OWL BLOCK

1 Using the instructions on page 191, or your favourite method, Foundation Paper Piece the individual sections of Oscar.

2 Referencing Figure 1, join together in the following order:

JOIN THE SECTIONS:

E + F
EF + C
EFC + A
EFCA + I
EFCAI + L
EFCAIL + M

JOIN THE SECTIONS:

G + H
GH+ D
GHD + B
GHDB + J
GHDBJ + K
GHDBJK + N

JOIN THE SECTIONS:

EFCAILM + GHDBJKN

3 Remove the papers and press.

ATTACHING THE BORDERS

1 Join the shorter Wiltshire Shade Blue Borders to the left and right of the Oscar Owl block and press towards the Border. Join the longer Wiltshire Shade Blue Borders to the top and bottom. Press towards the Border.

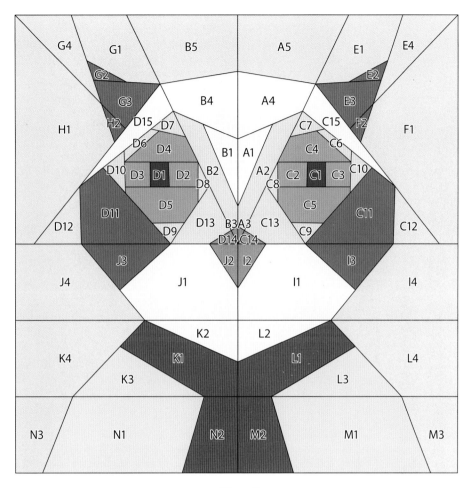

Figure 1

2 Repeat Step 1, joining the Arthur's Ark Light Blue Borders. (Fig. 2)

QUILT

Position and secure the quilt top to the batting and quilt around the Owl head and main features using a 12wt thread to accentuate them. I used a blue and an orange to add a little more definition around some of the shapes. Trim the quilted pillow top to 22½" square.

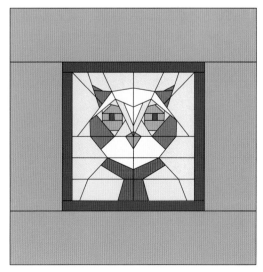

Figure 2

ASSEMBLING THE PILLOW

1 Make a double hem on one 22½" side of each of your backing rectangles by folding one 22½" edge in ¼" and pressing with an iron. Fold the edge in another ¼" and press. Topstitch ⅛" away from the folded edge and press. (Fig. 3)

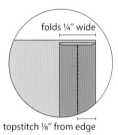

folds ¼" wide

topstitch ⅛" from edge

Figure 3

2 Lay your finished pillow Front right side facing up. With the right sides together, align a double hemmed 18½" × 22½" backing rectangle with three raw edges of the pillow Front. (Fig. 4)

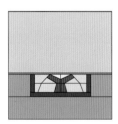

Figure 4

3 Align a double hemmed 18½" × 22½" backing rectangle along the opposite edge of the pillow Front. The backing rectangles will overlap. (Fig. 5)

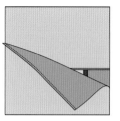

Figure 5

4 Pin around all four sides and sew using a ¼" seam. Trim the corners to remove some of the bulk, being careful not to cut into the seam.

5 Turn the pillow right side out, press, and place a 24" square pillow insert inside the pillow sleeve.

TIP: *Using a slightly larger pillow form than your finished cushion sleeve will help your pillow keep its shape over time.*

A beautiful poem written by Gabrielle Djanogly tells the Owl's story:

> I've never liked the rain or snow,
> I'm frightened of the dark.
> It's why I'm perched at Liberty
> And not at Regent's Park.
> The third floor suits me to a tee,
> There's space to stretch my wings.
> And every year with Christmas near,
> The stars are hung on strings.

BLAKE

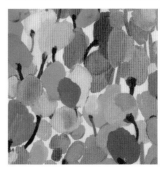

From top: Blake, Sun Daisy, Tulip Fields.

Liberty and London are synonymous; one immediately brings the other to mind. The United Kingdom's Capital has been the company's home for 145 years. The culture, fashion, architecture and people of London are a daily source of inspiration for the design team and the From London with Love seasonal collection for Spring/Summer 2020 draws upon this. The Tana Lawn prints are a visual journey through the city from Covent Garden to Bishopsgate, Hackney to Walthamstow and Bloomsbury to Regent Street.

I was lucky enough to have a preview of the collection when writing this book and the story of one particular design entitled Blake captured my imagination.

Blake is a print inspired by the patterns created by light filtering through the lead work in the glass of the Liberty Store and the diamond shapes have highlights of colour knitting it together. Back in 1875 each of the leaded windows had a small painted picture in one pane. I love that the character of the building is still a catalyst for print designs in the twenty first century.

I transformed this geometric fabric design into a modern quilt which is constructed in diamonds with Foundation Paper Piecing. These are perfect to showcase bold and bright prints and to bring a burst of Liberty colour into your living space. The Blake print features uninterrupted on the quilt back, bound with solid black Tana Lawn.

All of these fabrics are new to Liberty in 2020, some may return as part of the Liberty Classics collection in the future, or they may not be repeated and that is what makes it so hard not to collect them!

BLAKE

Finished Quilt Size: 45½" × 56¾" • *Finished Block Size:* 11¼" × 7½"

MATERIALS

Lexie A: 1 yard (91 cm)

Lauder Pink: ¾ yard (69 cm)

Petal Wish Turquoise: ½ yard (46 cm)

Tana Lawn Black: 1⅛ yard (1.03 m)

Tana Lawn White: ¼ yard (23 cm)

Sun Daisy Yellow: ¾ yard (69 cm)

Little Love Pink: ¾ yard (69 cm)

Tulip Fields B: ½ yard (46 cm)

Blake C: 1¾ yards for the backing

Tana Lawn Black: ½ yard (46 cm) for the binding

Batting: 54" × 65" (1.37 m × 1.65 m)

Templates (see pages 198–202)

CUTTING

From the Lexie A, cut:
(5) 5½" × 52" strips, subcut into:
> (25) 5½" × 7" rectangles (A1, D1)
>
> (4) 5½" × 4" rectangles (E1)
>
> (1) 5½" × 3½" rectangle (K1)

(4) 5" × 6" rectangles (F1)

(1) 4" × 6" rectangle (I1)

(1) 4¼" × 4" rectangle (H2)

(1) 4" × 2½" rectangle (J2)

(1) 3½" × 52" strip, subcut into:
> (5) 3½" × 7" rectangles (G2)

From the Lauder Pink, cut:
(3) 7" × 52" strips, subcut into:
> (25) 7" × 4" rectangles (A4, G1)
>
> (1) 6" × 2½" rectangle (J1)
>
> (1) 3" × 4" rectangle (H1)

From the Petal Wish Turquoise, cut:
(2) 8" × 52" strips, subcut into:
> (30) 8" × 2½" rectangles (A3, D3, F2, I2)
>
> (5) 3" × 2" rectangles (E3, K3)

From the Tana Lawn Black, cut:
(2) 9" × 52" strips, subcut into:
> (29) 9" × 2" rectangles (A5, E5, G3)
>
> (5) 6" × 2" rectangles (D2)

(1) 6" × 52" strip, subcut into:
> (25) 6" × 2" rectangles (A2, E2, K2)

(2) 3" × 52" strips, subcut into:
> (30) 3" × 1½" rectangles (C3)
>
> (5) 2" × 2" squares (F4, H3)
>
> (1) 2" × 8" rectangle (J3)

(1) 4½" × 52" strip, subcut into:
> (30) 4½" × 1½" rectangles (C2)

From the Tana Lawn White, cut:
(1) 3" × 52" strip, subcut into:
> (30) 3" × 1½" rectangles (C1)

From the Sun Daisy Yellow, cut:
(3) 8" × 52" strips, subcut into:
> (30) 8" × 4" rectangles (B2)

From the Little Love Pink, cut:
(3) 8" × 52" strips, subcut into:
> (30) 8" × 3½" rectangles (B1)

From the Tulip Fields B, cut:
(2) 8" × 52" strips subcut into:
> (30) 8" × 2½" rectangles (B3)

ASSEMBLING THE BLOCKS

1 Using the instructions on page 191, Foundation Paper Piece (FPP) the individual sections, referencing Figure 1 for fabric placement.

2 Make a total of 20 A, 30 B, 30 C, 5 D, 4 E, 4 F, 5 G, 1 H, 1 I, 1 J, and 1 K blocks.

3 Referencing Figure 1, join sections B and C, matching the seams.

ASSEMBLING THE QUILT TOP

1 Referencing Figure 2, join the blocks together in rows.

2 Join the rows.

3 Remove the papers.

QUILT

The Blake quilt has been quilted on a domestic machine. Because the main print is so bold, I felt it didn't require dense quilting so I stitched-in-the-ditch using a contrasting pink thread.

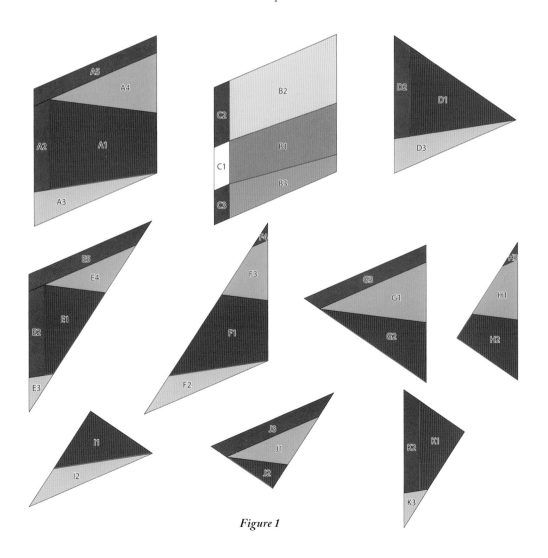

Figure 1

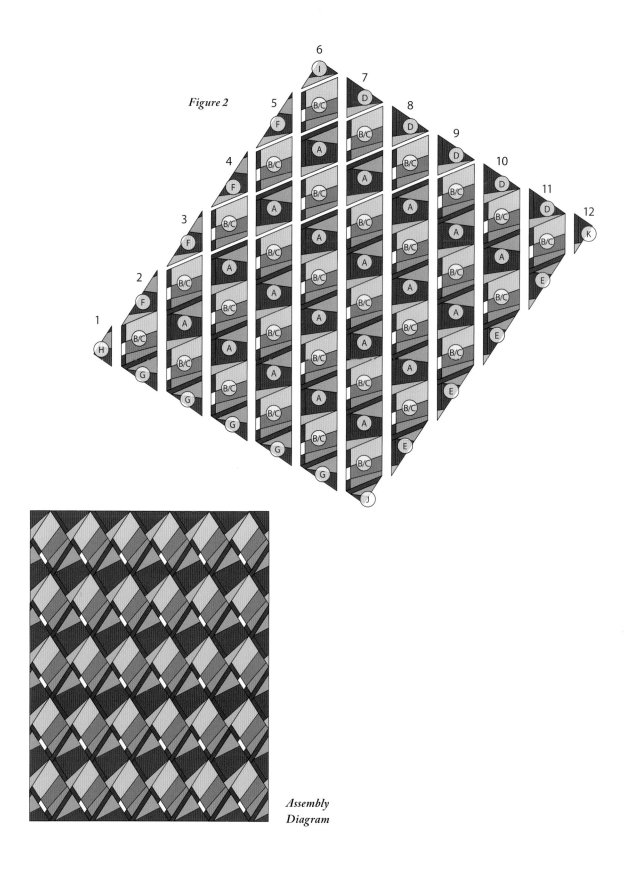

Figure 2

Assembly Diagram

BISHOPSGATE

The final quilt project starts with current Liberty Fabric designs. These take us back to the traditional skill of English Paper Piecing, which was applied by sewists in the UK, many years before the Liberty Fabrics story began. Today, quilters across the world love to create intricate designs using Liberty motifs and geometric shapes. The Bishopsgate print, also in the From London with Love Collection, revealed itself as the perfect template to recreate in this medium. Bishopsgate is a monochrome screen-printed design featuring circles merging together, inspired by the kaleidoscope of lines created in the reflections of the busy skyline of the City of London. One complete Bishopsgate Rosette contains 176 paper pieces, so this is a brilliant project to take with you on the go and to work on a little bit at a time.

Fussy-cutting is the practice of focusing on a single area of a print and cutting out a shape to use in a specific quilt block. Historical examples of this practice exist in antique quilts, but it has recently become very fashionable amongst sewists with Instagram sew-alongs and challenges. Liberty is the dream fabric for fussy-cutters as it is packed with so many fascinating details and I encourage everybody to give it a try. I chose to highlight the birds from Chrissy and butterflies in Downshire Hill as well as using Bishopsgate in the centre to recreate a new geometric design. But this project will look fantastic in so many combinations of Liberty prints, both old and new.

There is an ongoing debate whether or not quilting is Art, but as I stitched this project I was really struck by its beauty and so I have chosen to frame it for display on a wall. It would also make a beautiful mini quilt or cushion once appliquéd onto a background fabric.

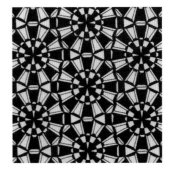

From top: Bishopsgate, Chrissy, Downshire Hill.

BISHOPSGATE

Finished Quilt Size: 20" square

MATERIALS

¼ yard (23 cm) from *Bishopsgate Blue, Downshire Hill Blue, Little Love Blue, Pauline Marie Blue, Chrissy Yellow,* and *Glimmer Blue*

Bishopsgate Blue: ¾ yard (69 cm) for background mount

Templates (see page 197)

Template Plastic

Light cardstock (approx. 160 gsm or #80)

Heavyweight 23" (58 cm) square board for mounting

Glue pen

PVA glue and brush

Quilting clips

KEY

A = Bishopsgate Blue

B = Downshire Hill Blue

C, C rev, E, E rev, G, G rev = Little Love Blue

D = Pauline Marie Blue

F = Chrissy Yellow

H = Glimmer Blue

ASSEMBLING THE UNITS

1 Trace the patterns on page 197 onto template plastic.

2 Trace around the templates onto light cardstock for a total of 11 shapes.

3 Using the template plastic, draw around the templates on the wrong side of the fabric. Cut out the shapes from the fabric including roughly an additional ¼" for the seam allowance. Fussy cut the butterfly from Downshire Hill Blue, the bird from Chrissy Yellow and the Bishopsgate Blue if desired.

4 Baste the individual fabric shapes onto the card pieces using a glue pen. (Fig. 1). EPP and hand sewing tips can be found in the Quilt Making Basics section (pages 187–191).

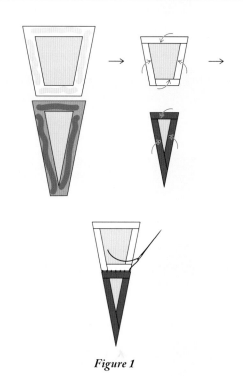

Figure 1

5 Join the sections in the following order:

A + B
C + D + C rev
E + F + E rev
G + H + G rev
AB + CDC
ABCDC + EFE
ABCDCEFE + GHG

TIP: *When joining pieces, hold them together with a quilting clip to prevent the shapes moving out of place whilst sewing.*

6 Repeat Steps 1–5 to make a total of 16 wedge units. (Fig. 2)

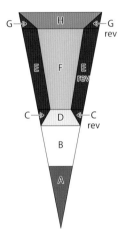

Figure 2

7 Join the wedge units into two semi-circle halves. (Fig. 3)

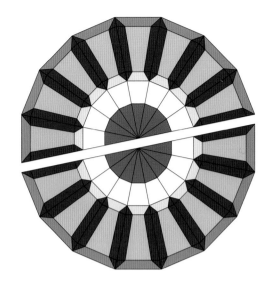

Figure 3

8 Join the two halves of the rosette.

9 Leave the card pieces in situ and secure any tails to the back of the units using fabric glue.

10 Mount the rosette onto a 23" square board using PVA glue.

11 Our Bishopsgate rosette is additionally mounted onto a 27" square background of Bishopsgate Blue fabric which has been bonded to cardstock by a professional art framer.

THE SWATCHES

This index is organized by project and will help you quickly identify the fabrics used in each and allow you to compare with substitute fabrics should you wish. When purchasing fabric from Liberty or an authorized retailer, use only the fabric name and letter suffix or the code listed below. Please note that not all prints are to scale.

KEY: T = Tana Lawn; L = Lasenby Cotton

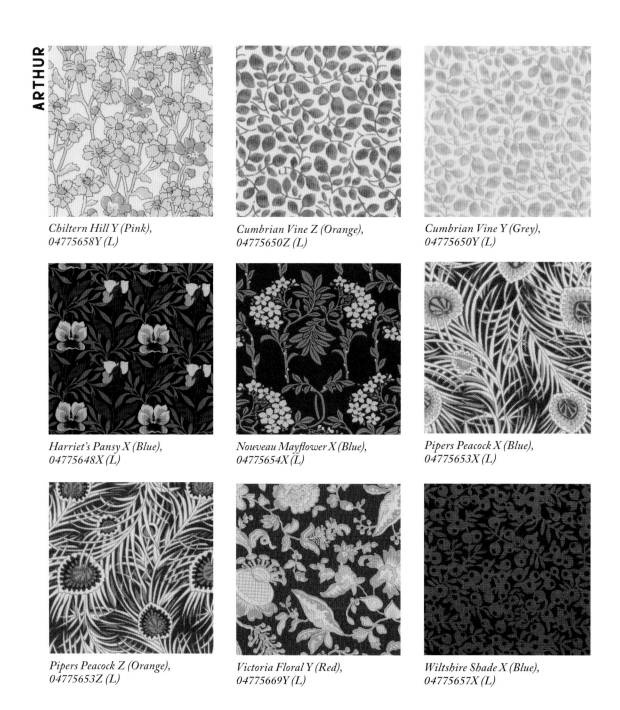

ARTHUR

Chiltern Hill Y (Pink), 04775658Y (L)

Cumbrian Vine Z (Orange), 04775650Z (L)

Cumbrian Vine Y (Grey), 04775650Y (L)

Harriet's Pansy X (Blue), 04775648X (L)

Nouveau Mayflower X (Blue), 04775654X (L)

Pipers Peacock X (Blue), 04775653X (L)

Pipers Peacock Z (Orange), 04775653Z (L)

Victoria Floral Y (Red), 04775669Y (L)

Wiltshire Shade X (Blue), 04775657X (L)

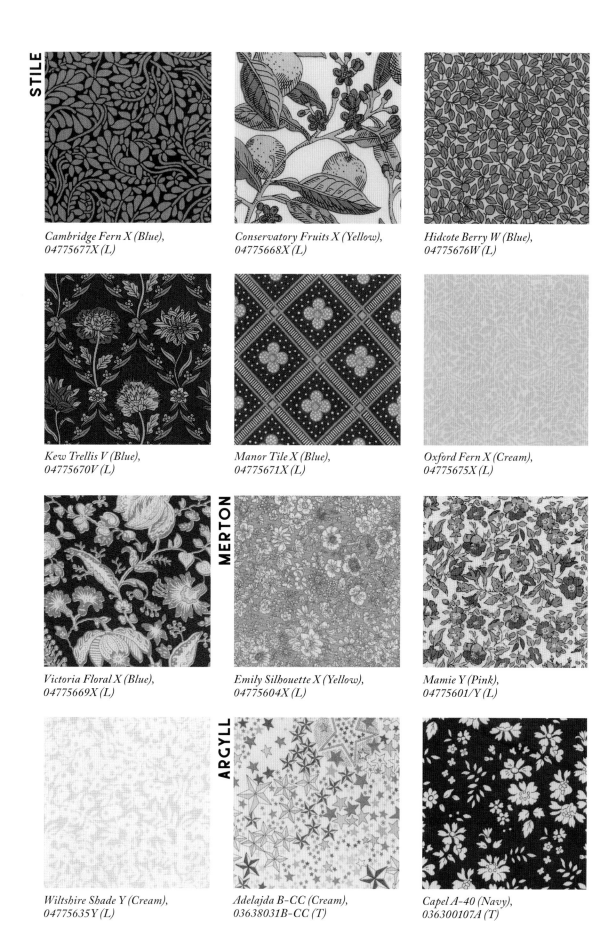

STILE

Cambridge Fern X (Blue), 04775677X (L)

Conservatory Fruits X (Yellow), 04775668X (L)

Hidcote Berry W (Blue), 04775676W (L)

Kew Trellis V (Blue), 04775670V (L)

Manor Tile X (Blue), 04775671X (L)

Oxford Fern X (Cream), 04775675X (L)

MERTON

Victoria Floral X (Blue), 04775669X (L)

Emily Silhouette X (Yellow), 04775604X (L)

Mamie Y (Pink), 04775601/Y (L)

ARGYLL

Wiltshire Shade Y (Cream), 04775635Y (L)

Adelajda B-CC (Cream), 03638031B-CC (T)

Capel A-40 (Navy), 036300107A (T)

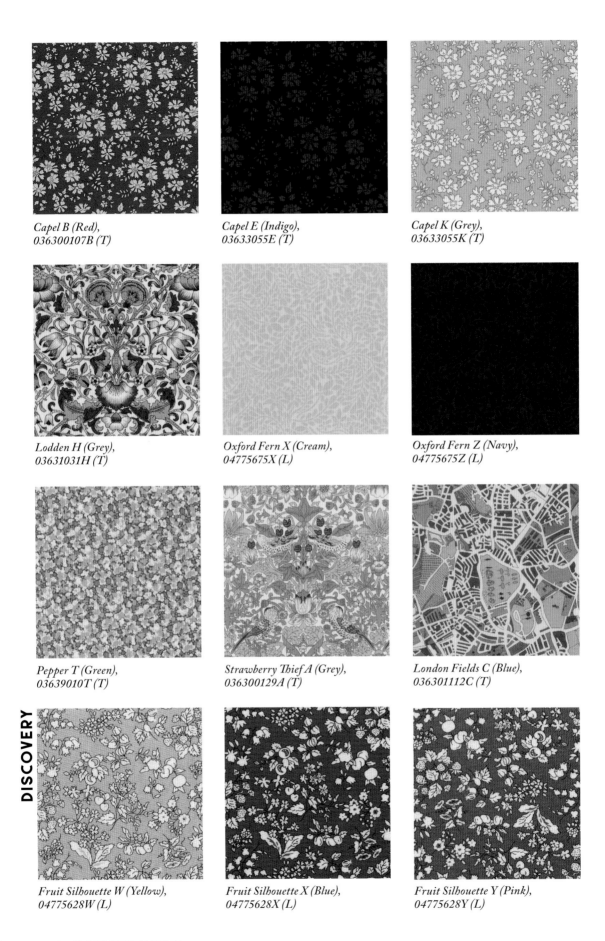

Capel B (Red),
036300107B (T)

Capel E (Indigo),
03633055E (T)

Capel K (Grey),
03633055K (T)

Lodden H (Grey),
03631031H (T)

Oxford Fern X (Cream),
04775675X (L)

Oxford Fern Z (Navy),
04775675Z (L)

Pepper T (Green),
03639010T (T)

Strawberry Thief A (Grey),
036300129A (T)

London Fields C (Blue),
036301112C (T)

Fruit Silhouette W (Yellow),
04775628W (L)

Fruit Silhouette X (Blue),
04775628X (L)

Fruit Silhouette Y (Pink),
04775628Y (L)

DISCOVERY

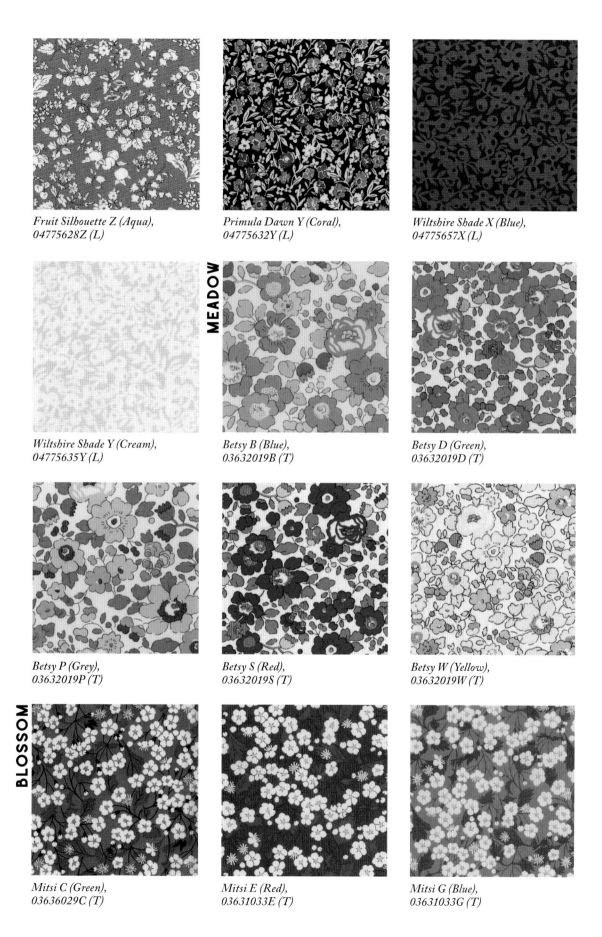

Fruit Silhouette Z (Aqua),
04775628Z (L)

Primula Dawn Y (Coral),
04775632Y (L)

Wiltshire Shade X (Blue),
04775657X (L)

MEADOW

Wiltshire Shade Y (Cream),
04775635Y (L)

Betsy B (Blue),
03632019B (T)

Betsy D (Green),
03632019D (T)

Betsy P (Grey),
03632019P (T)

Betsy S (Red),
03632019S (T)

Betsy W (Yellow),
03632019W (T)

BLOSSOM

Mitsi C (Green),
03636029C (T)

Mitsi E (Red),
03631033E (T)

Mitsi G (Blue),
03631033G (T)

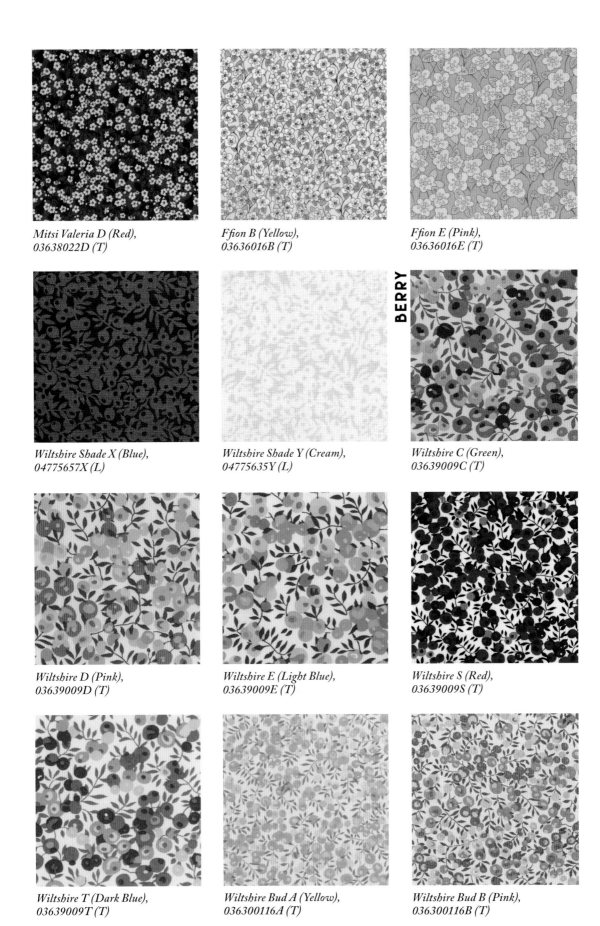

Mitsi Valeria D (Red),
03638022D (T)

Ffion B (Yellow),
03636016B (T)

Ffion E (Pink),
03636016E (T)

Wiltshire Shade X (Blue),
04775657X (L)

Wiltshire Shade Y (Cream),
04775635Y (L)

BERRY

Wiltshire C (Green),
03639009C (T)

Wiltshire D (Pink),
03639009D (T)

Wiltshire E (Light Blue),
03639009E (T)

Wiltshire S (Red),
03639009S (T)

Wiltshire T (Dark Blue),
03639009T (T)

Wiltshire Bud A (Yellow),
036300116A (T)

Wiltshire Bud B (Pink),
036300116B (T)

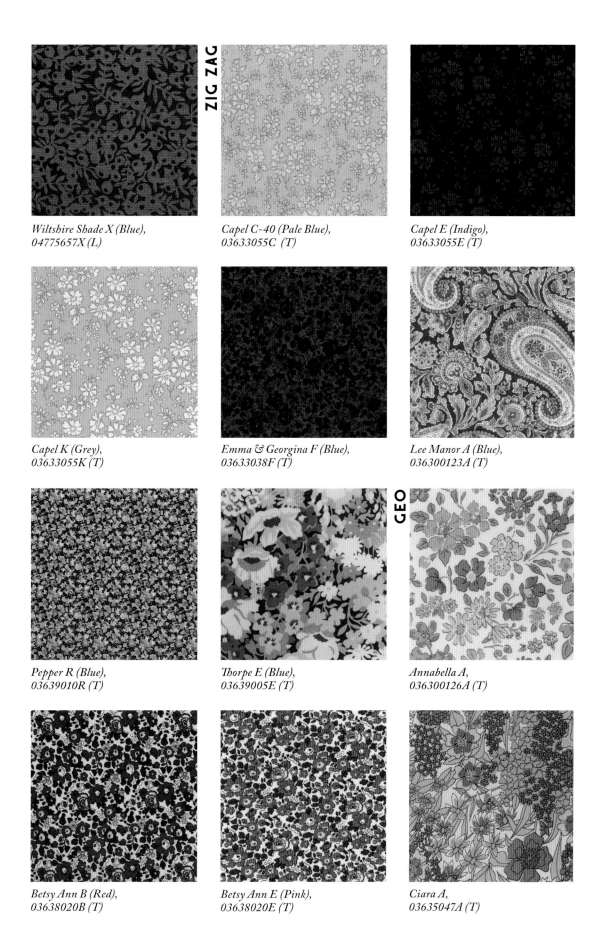

ZIG ZAG

Wiltshire Shade X (Blue),
04775657X (L)

Capel C-40 (Pale Blue),
03633055C (T)

Capel E (Indigo),
03633055E (T)

Capel K (Grey),
03633055K (T)

Emma & Georgina F (Blue),
03633038F (T)

Lee Manor A (Blue),
036300123A (T)

GEO

Pepper R (Blue),
03639010R (T)

Thorpe E (Blue),
03639005E (T)

Annabella A,
036300126A (T)

Betsy Ann B (Red),
03638020B (T)

Betsy Ann E (Pink),
03638020E (T)

Ciara A,
03635047A (T)

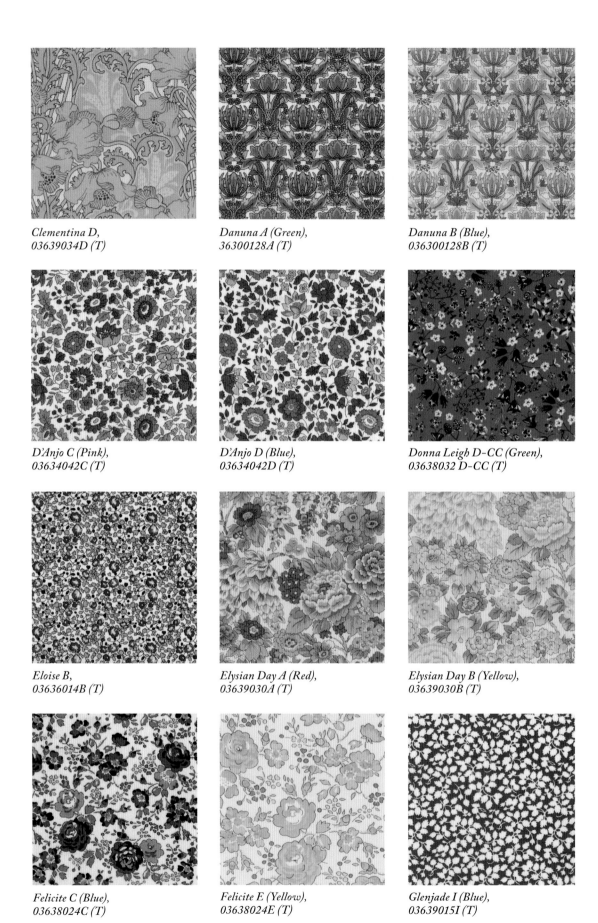

Clementina D,
03639034D (T)

Danuna A (Green),
36300128A (T)

Danuna B (Blue),
036300128B (T)

D'Anjo C (Pink),
03634042C (T)

D'Anjo D (Blue),
03634042D (T)

Donna Leigh D–CC (Green),
03638032 D–CC (T)

Eloise B,
03636014B (T)

Elysian Day A (Red),
03639030A (T)

Elysian Day B (Yellow),
03639030B (T)

Felicite C (Blue),
03638024C (T)

Felicite E (Yellow),
03638024E (T)

Glenjade I (Blue),
03639015I (T)

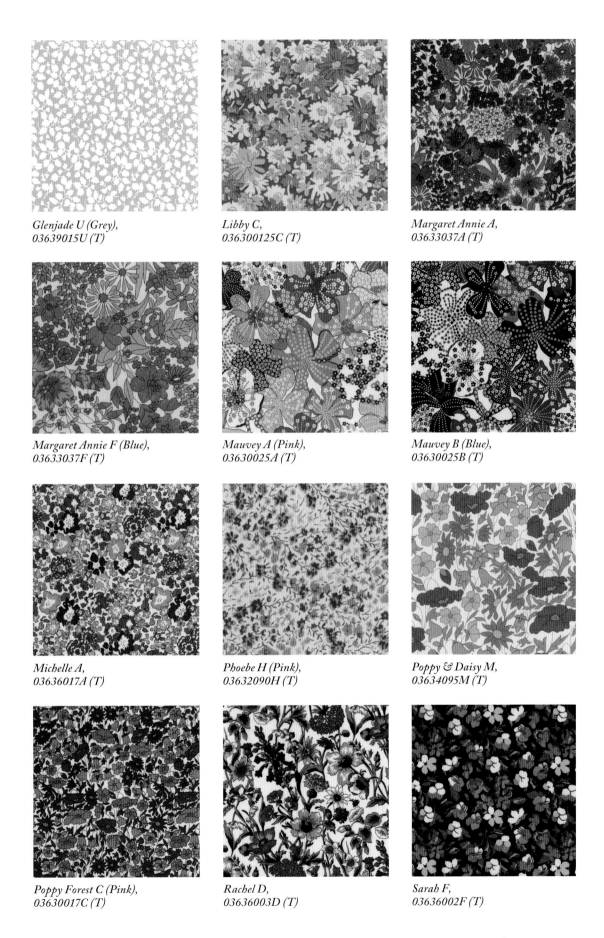

Glenjade U (Grey),
03639015U (T)

Libby C,
036300125C (T)

Margaret Annie A,
03633037A (T)

Margaret Annie F (Blue),
03633037F (T)

Mauvey A (Pink),
03630025A (T)

Mauvey B (Blue),
03630025B (T)

Michelle A,
03636017A (T)

Phoebe H (Pink),
03632090H (T)

Poppy & Daisy M,
03634095M (T)

Poppy Forest C (Pink),
03630017C (T)

Rachel D,
03636003D (T)

Sarah F,
03636002F (T)

Swirling Petals A (Red),
036390124A (T)

Tatum K,
03631082K (T)

Thorpe Hill C,
036300115C (T)

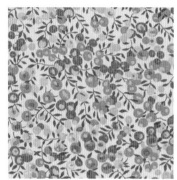

LOVE AND KISSES

Tresco A-CC,
03633185A-CC (T)

Wiltshire Bud B (Pink),
036300116B (T)

Little Love C (Red),
036301140C (T)

OSCAR OWL

Oxford Fern Y (Pink),
04775675Y (L)

Wiltshire Shade Y (Cream),
04775635Y (L)

Adelajda B-CC (Cream),
03638031B-CC (T)

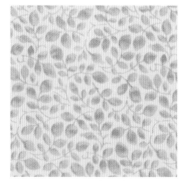

Arthur's Ark Z (Light Blue),
036357443Z (T)

Cambridge Fern X,
04775677X (L)

Cumbrian Vine X (Blue),
04775650X (L)

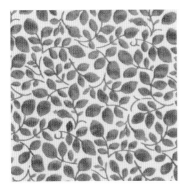

Cumbrian Vine Z (Orange),
04775650Z (L)

Feather Dance X (Blue),
04775673X (L)

Feather Dance Y (Orange),
04775673Y (L)

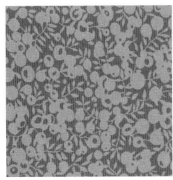

Wiltshire Shadow Z (Clementine),
04775682Z (L)

Wiltshire Shadow A (Silver Metallic),
04775755A (L)

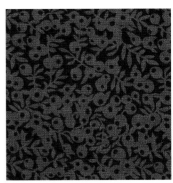

Wiltshire Shade X (Blue),
04775657X (L)

Blake C,
036301142C (T)

Lauder A,
036301129A (T)

Lexie A,
036300141A (T)

Little Love C,
036301140C (T)

Petal Wish A,
036301105A (T)

Sun Daisy C,
036301128C (T)

BLAKE

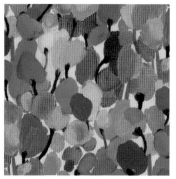

Tulip Fields B,
036301127B (T)

Bishopsgate B (Blue),
036301115B (T)

Chrissy A (Yellow),
036301144A (T)

Downshire Hill C,
036301120C (T)

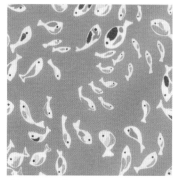

Glimmer C (Blue),
036301124C (T)

Little Love B,
036301140B (T)

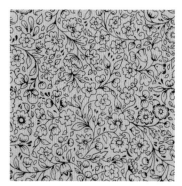

Pauline Marie C (Blue),
036301135C (T)

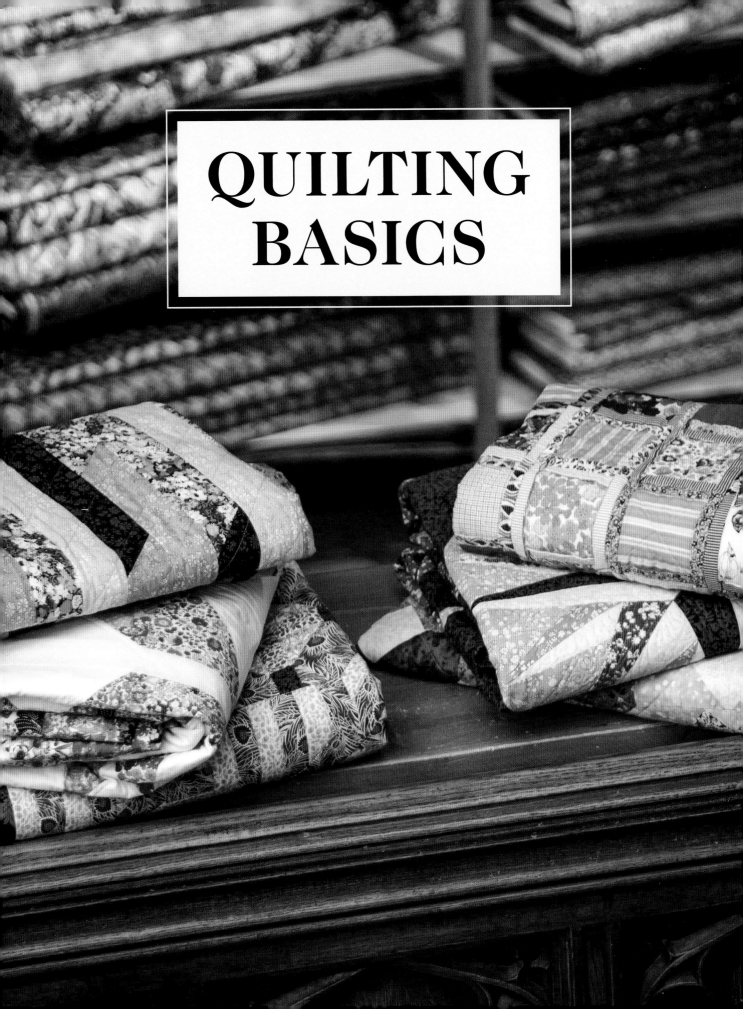

QUILTING BASICS

SEAM ALLOWANCE

The quilts in this book have been pieced using a ¼" seam allowance unless otherwise stated.

STITCH LENGTH

When piecing, use a stitch length of 2–2.4mm. For Foundation Paper Piecing use 1.8mm. When quilting with a walking foot use 3.0mm.

BASTING

Basting is when you use a temporary method of securing the three layers of the 'quilt sandwich' together. Spray basting is a quick method and works well with Lasenby Cotton but I would recommend hand basting Tana Lawn because of its delicate nature. Use a cotton basting thread which will not snag your quilt top when removed. Secure the layers in a grid formation with stitches every 3–5" from each other. (Fig. 1)

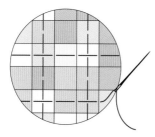

Figure 1

BINDING

All bindings in this book are 2½" wide and sewn on with ¼" seam allowance. This is important for the integrity of several quilt designs including Discovery, Berry, Love and Kisses and Blake (a ⅜" seam would be too wide for points at the quilt edge).

Join the binding with diagonal seams (Fig. 1) and finish by creating a 2½" overlap of the binding strips, joining on the diagonal then sewing and trimming. (Fig. 2)

Figure 1

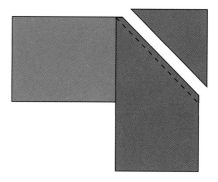

Figure 2

NEEDLETURN APPLIQUÉ

The Meadow Quilt uses the traditional technique of turning under the raw edges of appliqué shapes and stitching them to a backing fabric. It is important to cut from well-pressed fabric and to use sharp scissors when preparing your shapes. The method of applying freezer paper to the right side of the shape provides a clear visual guide when you are turning the fabric under to the wrong side before stitching. Use short appliqué pins to hold your shape in position before stitching. This will avoid getting your thread caught. The freezer paper is peeled away once the shape has been completed and can be re-used. Alternatively the shape can be hand basted to the background fabric, turning under a ¼" seam allowance and appliquéing. Use a 50wt or 80wt thread that blends well with your fabric.

APPLIQUÉING AT CONCAVE CURVES, CORNERS, AND POINTS

1 At concave curves, clip into the seam allowance ¹⁄₁₆" along the curve. The tighter the curve is, the more clips you will need. Space evenly for a more fluid curve.

2 At corners, fold each side under as you come to it to create a defined corner. Use extra stitches at the corner to secure.

At points such as the tips of a leaf, snip off the tip of the point leaving a scant ¼" seam allowance. Next fold under the excess seam allowance on the point so that it lays almost at a 90 degree angle to your stitches. Hold it in position until you reach the tip. Use extra, small stitches to secure it, then continue along the shape as before.

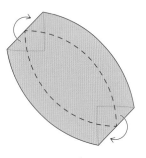

Figure 1

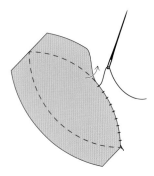

Figure 2

HAND SEWING KIT

Hand sewing can be made considerably easier by adopting just a few simple habits:

1 Keep your thread at a workable length — no longer than your wrist to elbow distance.

2 Apply a thread conditioner to minimise tangles.

3 Ensure the eye of your needle matches the width of the thread you are using. Now and again, adjust the position of the thread where it makes contact with the needle, to avoid any wear or snapping.

4 Make tidy knots such as a quilter's knot which will be less bulky to hide in the layers of a quilt.

5 Practice getting the right amount of tension, in your stitches. This is just as important when sewing by hand as it is when sewing on your machine.

6 Try to find a thimble that fits you comfortably. Persevere with it as it may take a few sessions to get used to it, but it can make hand sewing more comfortable in the long-term.

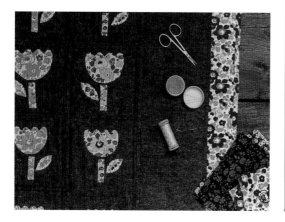

ENGLISH PAPER PIECING (EPP)

In the Bishopsgate Project it is suggested that you glue baste each of the sections. It is also possible to secure the fabric over the templates using a needle and thread. This is termed 'Thread Basting'.

HOW TO JOIN SHAPES TOGETHER

Place two basted shapes right sides together, aligning one edge. Pass your needle through the corner of two edges and make 2–3 stitches before passing the thread through the final loop made and pulling it taut to secure the stitches. Next whipstitch across the edge and secure the threads again at the end. The perfect whipstitch captures just a few threads on the fold of each fabric shape and is barely visible from the right side. A fine 50wt or 80wt thread that blends well with your fabric, will make this much easier.

FOUNDATION PAPER PIECING (FPP)

GETTING STARTED

Photocopy the required number of templates and cut out each template roughly, leaving space around it beyond the seam allowance if possible.

Be kind to yourself when cutting the piece of fabric you use for each section and ensure it is at least ¼" bigger on all sides.

PIECING ORDER

1 Choose unit A (see page 198) and fold a crease along the line between the 1st and 2nd sections, i.e. A1 and A2

2 Position another piece of fabric that will cover A1 with the wrong side facing down onto the non-printed side of the template. A window or lightbox can be helpful at this stage. Ensure it covers all of A1 with at least ¼" on all sides. Pin or glue in place.

3 Fold the paper back along the crease you made in step 1, and trim any excess fabric ¼" past the fold to create the seam allowance.

4 Cut a piece of fabric that will cover A2 again with at least ¼" extra on all sides. Line it up with the seam allowance of A1 with

the fabric right sides together and pin.

5 Unfold the paper, turn it over and sew along the line between A1 and A2. Begin at least ¼" before the line and finishing at least ¼" after. Use a stitch length of 1.8mm.

6 Open up the fabric and press.

7 Continue to add fabrics in the order of numbering, for example fold a line to A3 (please note that not all numbers are directly next to each other but keep moving to the next adjacent number). Trim the fabric ¼" past the fold to create the seam allowance and repeat steps 3 to 6.

8 Once all of the unit is covered, trim the seam allowance to the cutting line — note that if you use a rotary blade at this point it will gradually become blunted by the paper.

9 Repeat steps 1 to 7 for all units of the pattern.

10 Assemble the block according to the instructions, paying close attention to the order in which the units come together. Don't forget to pin at key points in the pattern where units need to align for the integrity of the design.

11 Remove the papers by tearing along the perforation stitch lines and press.

THE TEMPLATES

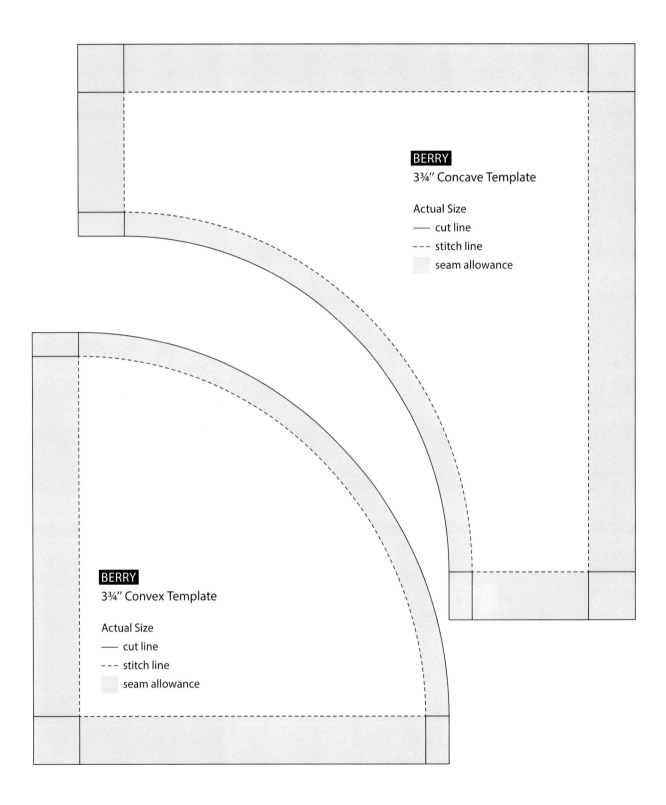

BERRY

3¾" Concave Template

Actual Size

— cut line

- - - stitch line

seam allowance

BERRY

3¾" Convex Template

Actual Size

— cut line

- - - stitch line

seam allowance

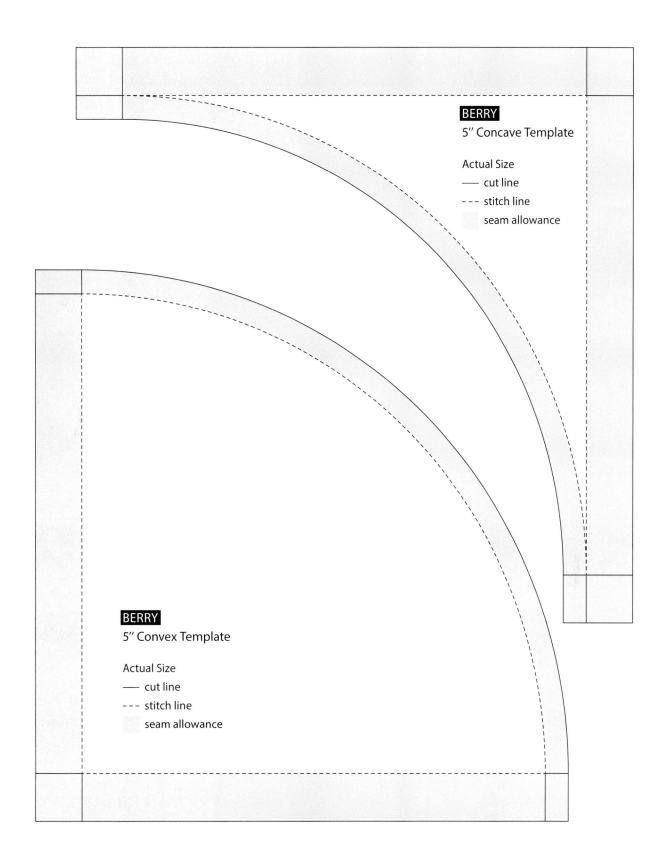

BERRY
5" Concave Template

Actual Size
— cut line
--- stitch line
seam allowance

BERRY
5" Convex Template

Actual Size
— cut line
--- stitch line
seam allowance

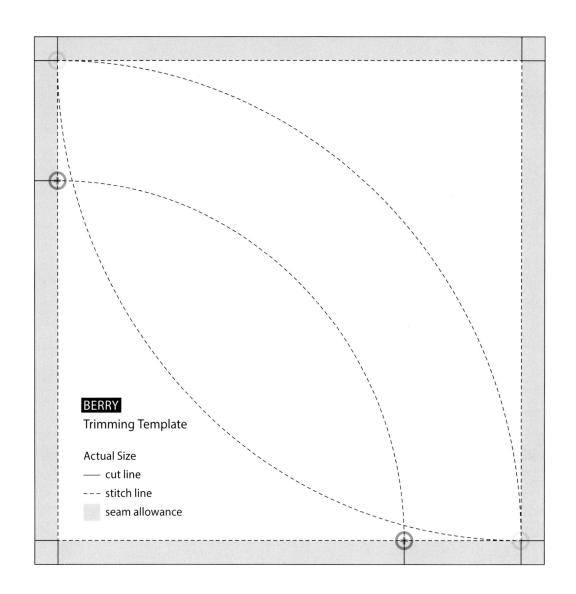

BERRY

Trimming Template

Actual Size

—— cut line

- - - stitch line

seam allowance

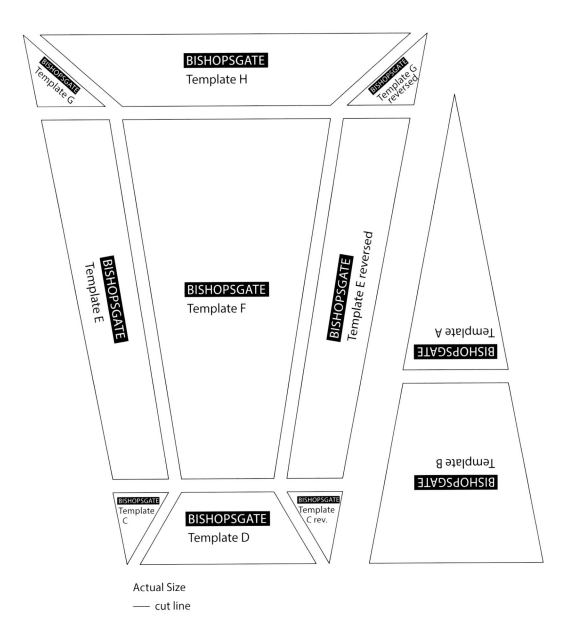

Actual Size

—— cut line

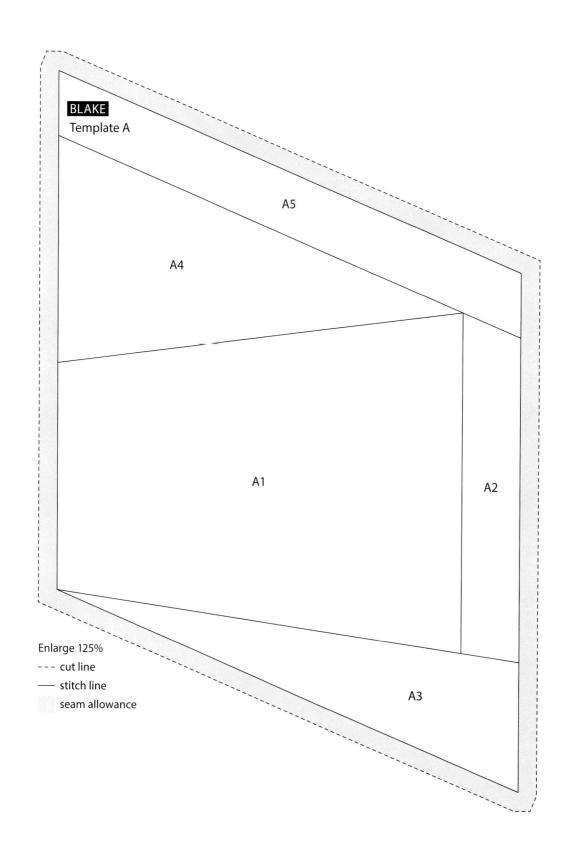

BLAKE
Template A

A5

A4

A1

A2

A3

Enlarge 125%
--- cut line
—— stitch line
    seam allowance

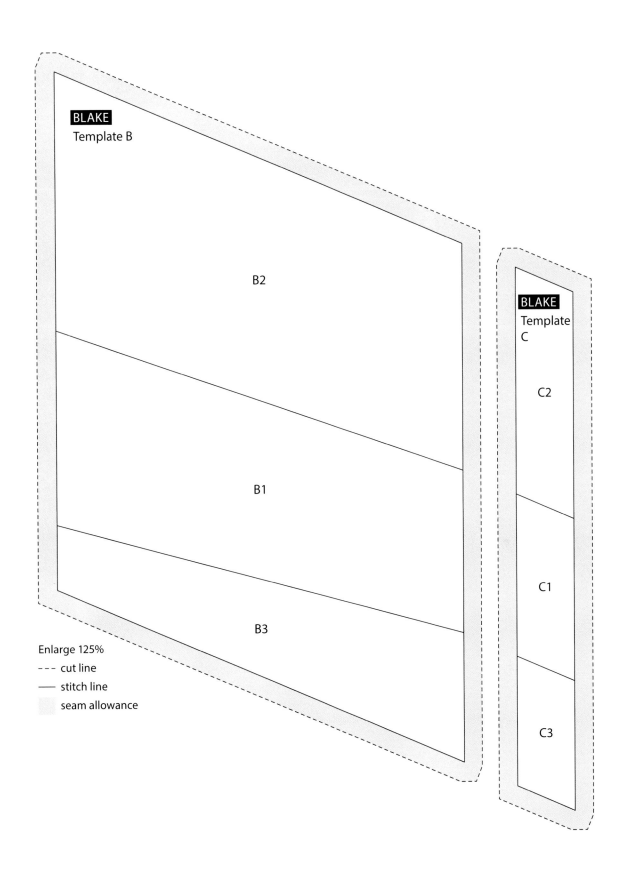

BLAKE
Template B

B2

B1

B3

BLAKE
Template
C

C2

C1

C3

Enlarge 125%

- - - cut line

—— stitch line

seam allowance

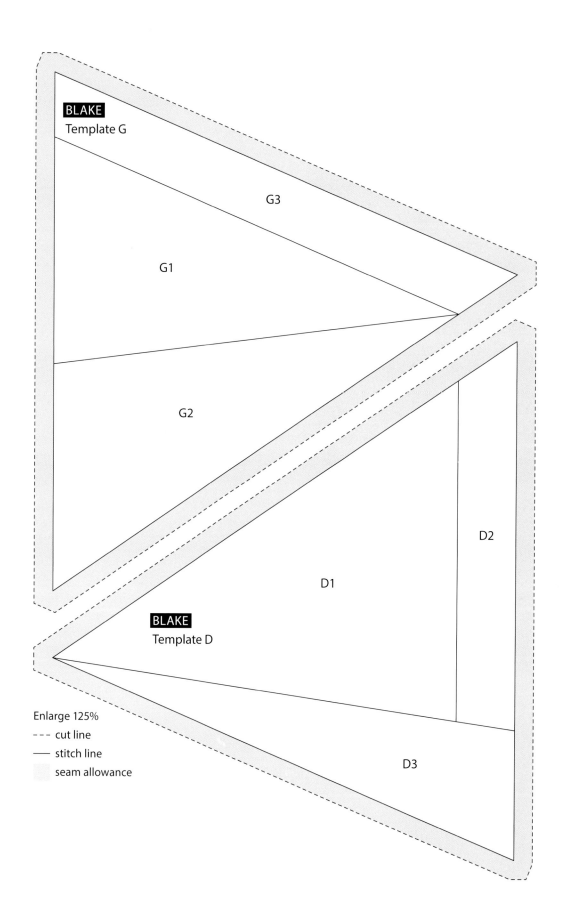

BLAKE
Template G

G3

G1

G2

D2

D1

BLAKE
Template D

D3

Enlarge 125%
- - - cut line
—— stitch line
seam allowance

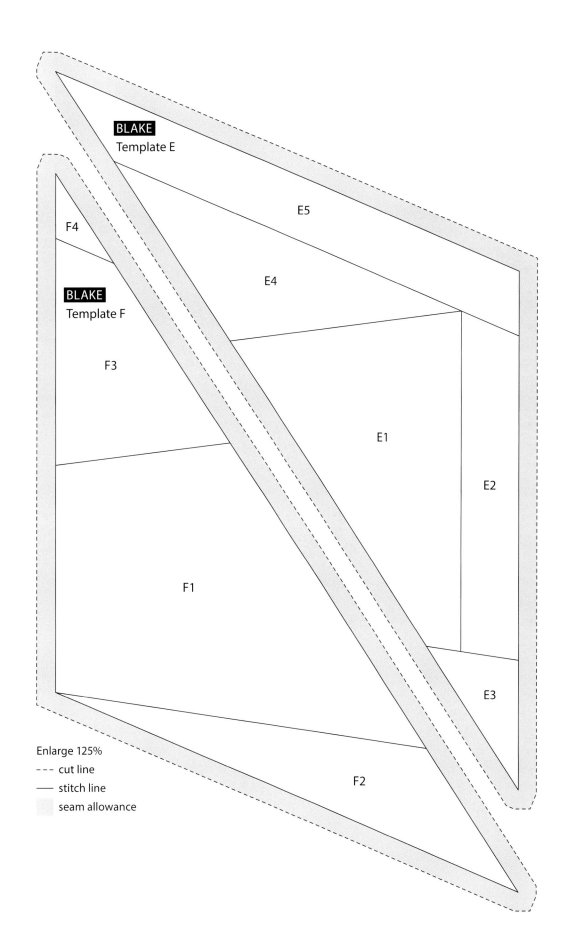

BLAKE
Template E

E5

F4

BLAKE
Template F

E4

F3

E1

E2

F1

E3

Enlarge 125%
- - - cut line
—— stitch line
█ seam allowance

F2

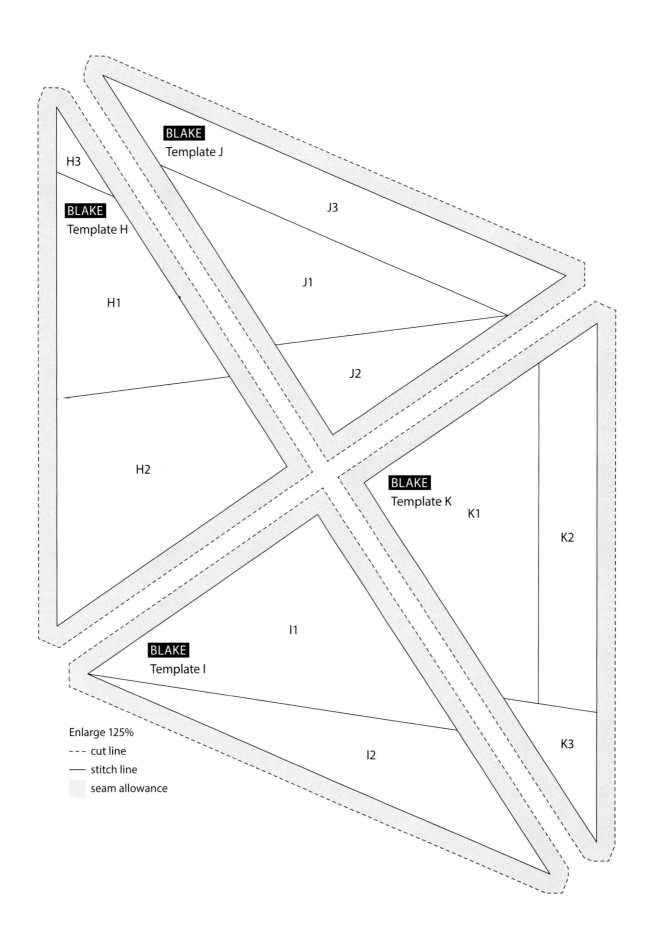

BLAKE
Template J

H3

BLAKE
Template H

J3

H1

J1

J2

H2

BLAKE
Template K

K1

K2

I1

BLAKE
Template I

Enlarge 125%
- - - cut line
—— stitch line
⬜ seam allowance

I2

K3

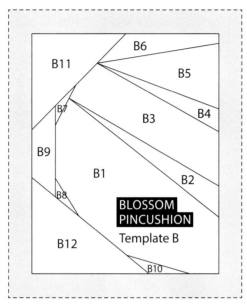

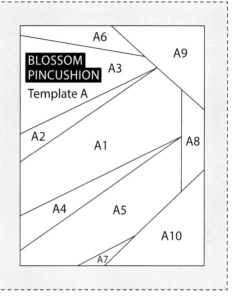

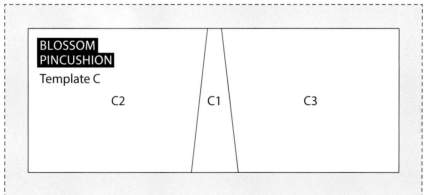

Actual Size

--- cut line

— stitch line

▨ seam allowance

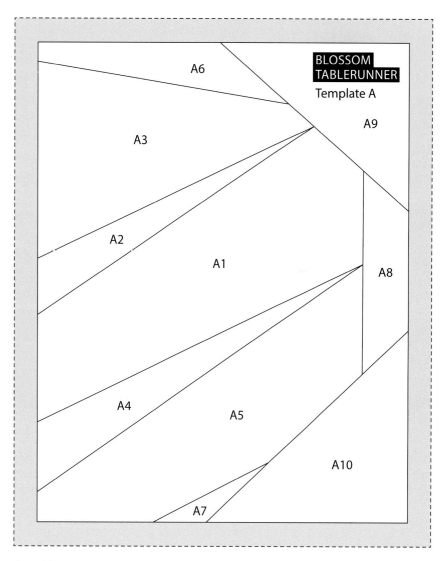

BLOSSOM
TABLERUNNER
Template A

A6

A9

A3

A2

A1

A8

A4

A5

A10

A7

Actual Size

--- cut line

—— stitch line

█ seam allowance

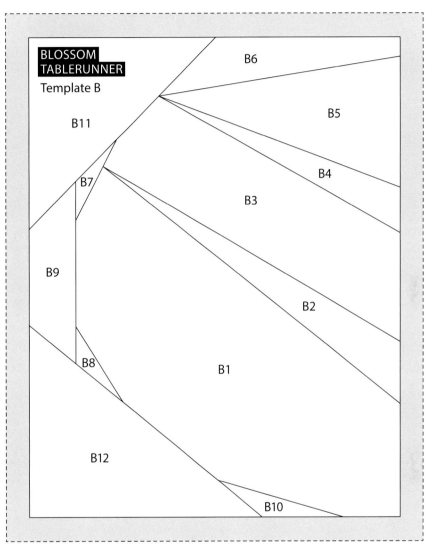

BLOSSOM
TABLERUNNER
Template B

B11

B6

B5

B4

B7

B3

B9

B2

B8

B1

B12

B10

Actual Size

--- cut line

—— stitch line

seam allowance

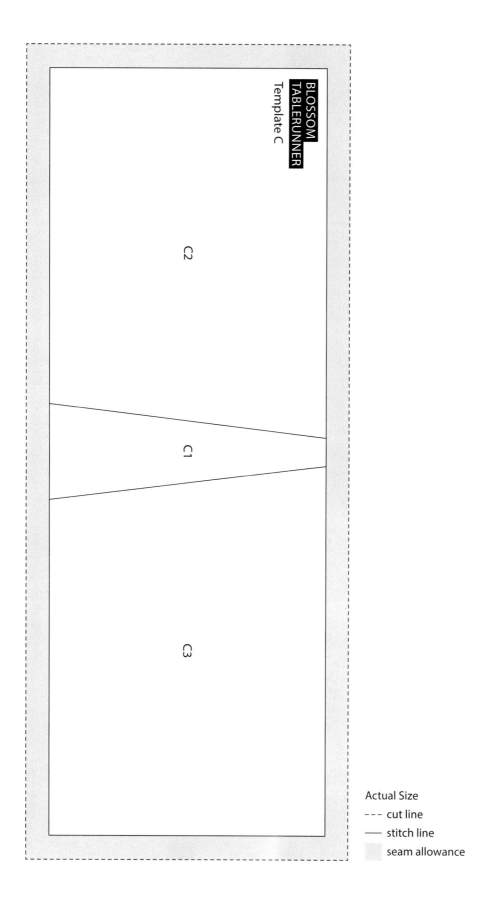

BLOSSOM
TABLERUNNER
Template C

C2

C1

C3

Actual Size

--- cut line

—— stitch line

▨ seam allowance

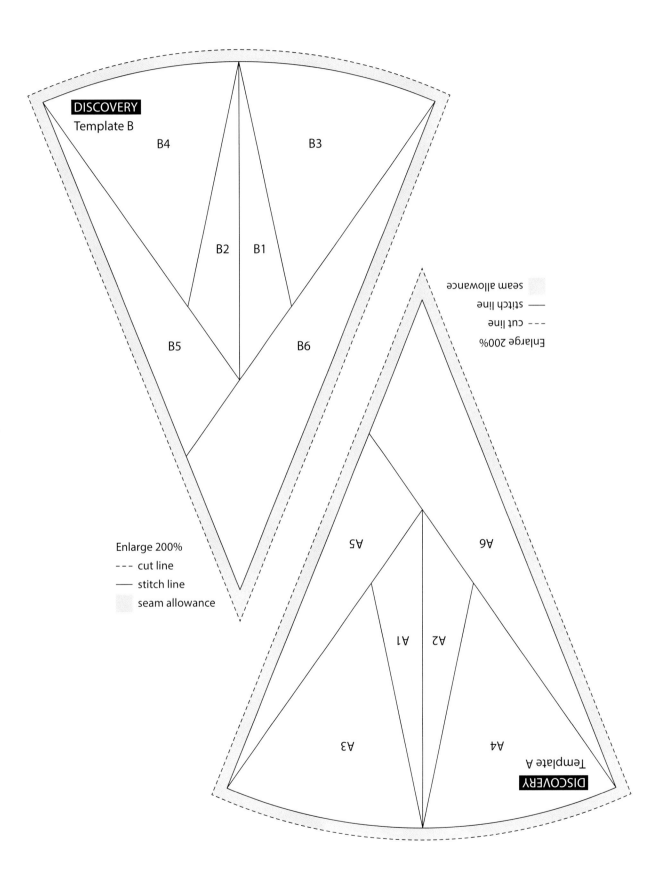

DISCOVERY
Template B

B4

B3

B2 | B1

B5

B6

Enlarge 200%
- - - cut line
——— stitch line
seam allowance

seam allowance
stitch line
cut line
Enlarge 200%

A5

A6

A1 | A2

A3

A4

Template A
DISCOVERY

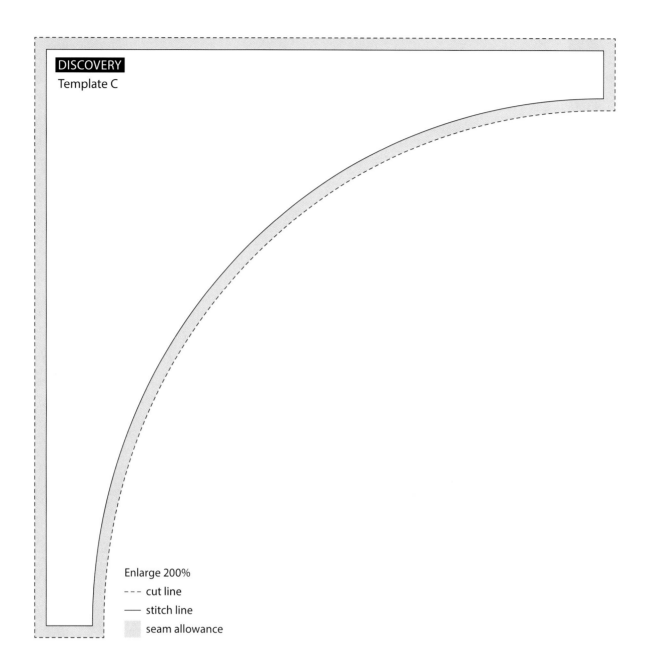

DISCOVERY
Template C

Enlarge 200%

- - - cut line

——— stitch line

▨ seam allowance

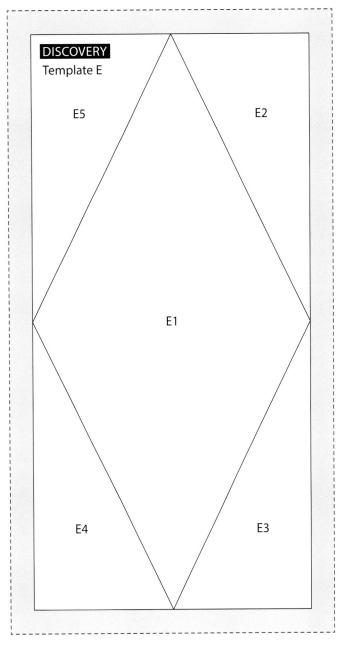

DISCOVERY
Template E

E5   E2

E1

E4   E3

Actual Size
--- cut line
— stitch line
seam allowance

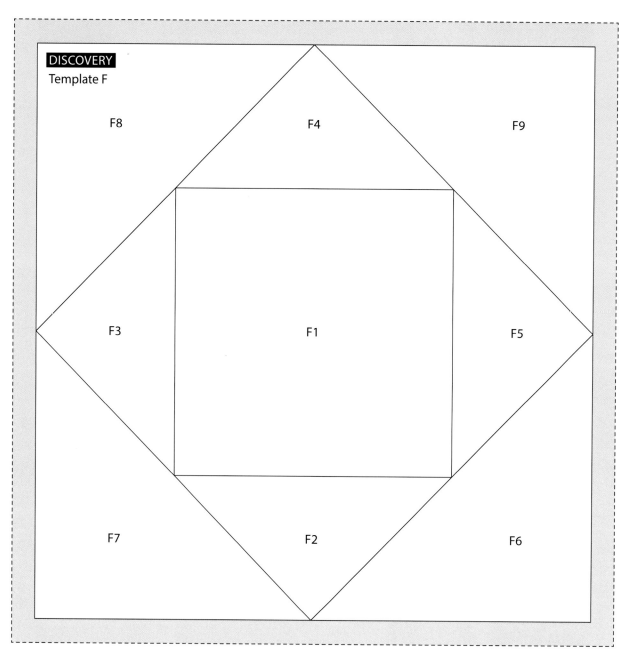

DISCOVERY
Template F

F8   F4   F9

F3   F1   F5

F7   F2   F6

Actual Size

--- cut line

—— stitch line

seam allowance

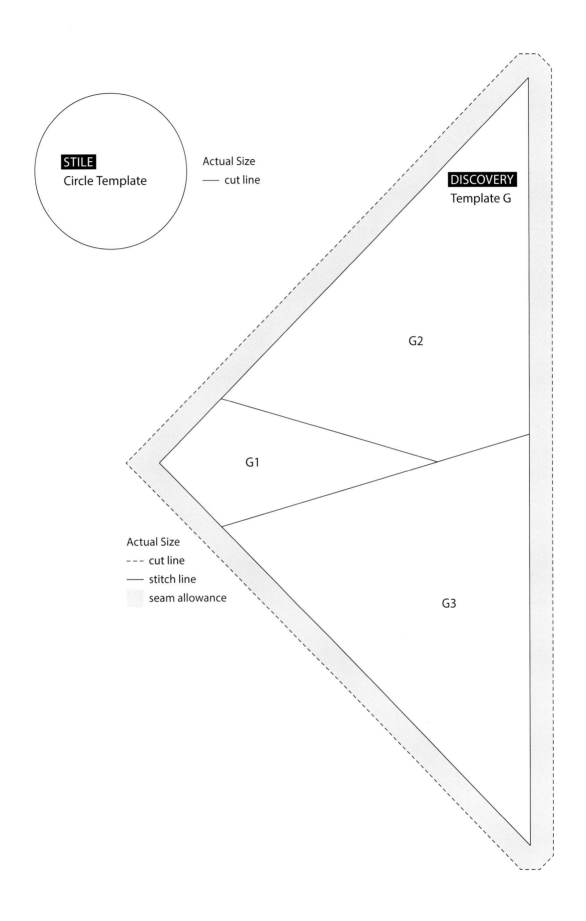

STILE
Circle Template

Actual Size
—— cut line

DISCOVERY
Template G

G2

G1

Actual Size
- - - cut line
—— stitch line
seam allowance

G3

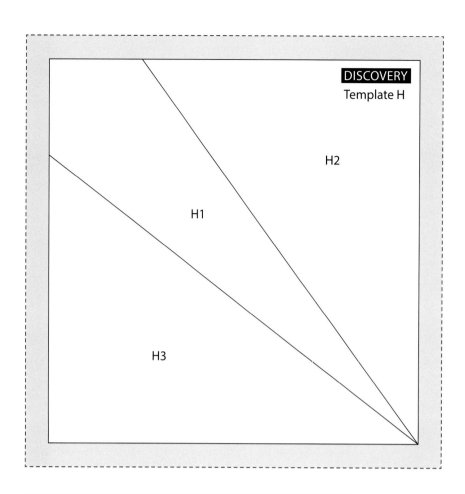

DISCOVERY
Template H

H2

H1

H3

Actual Size
- - - cut line
—— stitch line
     seam allowance

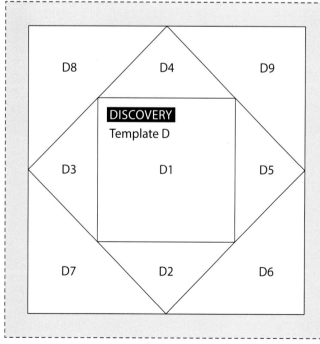

D8   D4   D9

DISCOVERY
Template D

D3   D1   D5

D7   D2   D6

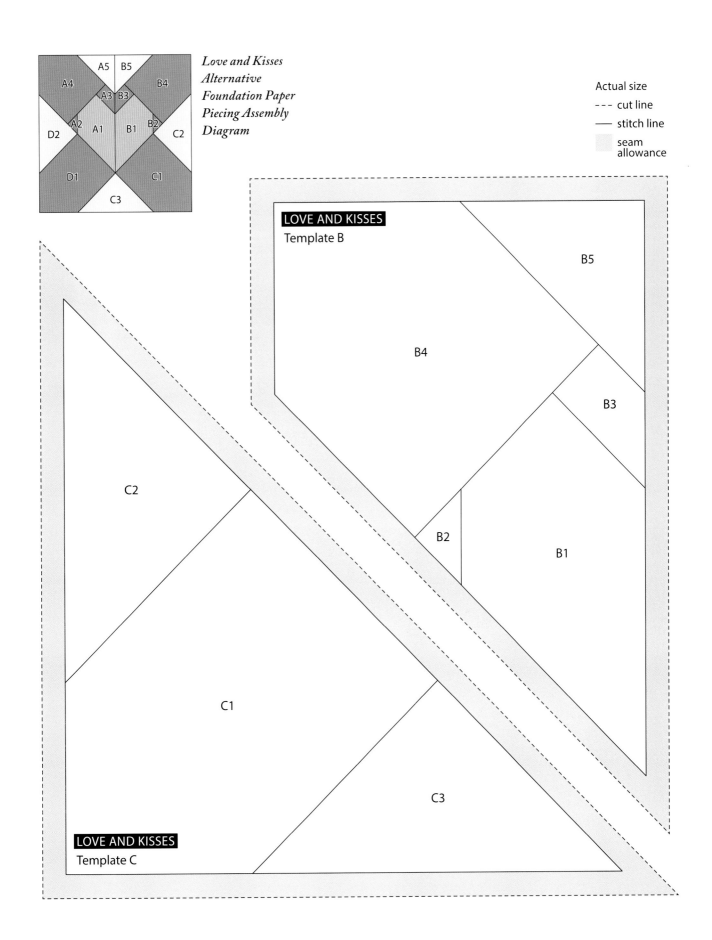

Love and Kisses
Alternative
Foundation Paper
Piecing Assembly
Diagram

Actual size
--- cut line
— stitch line
seam allowance

LOVE AND KISSES
Template B

LOVE AND KISSES
Template C

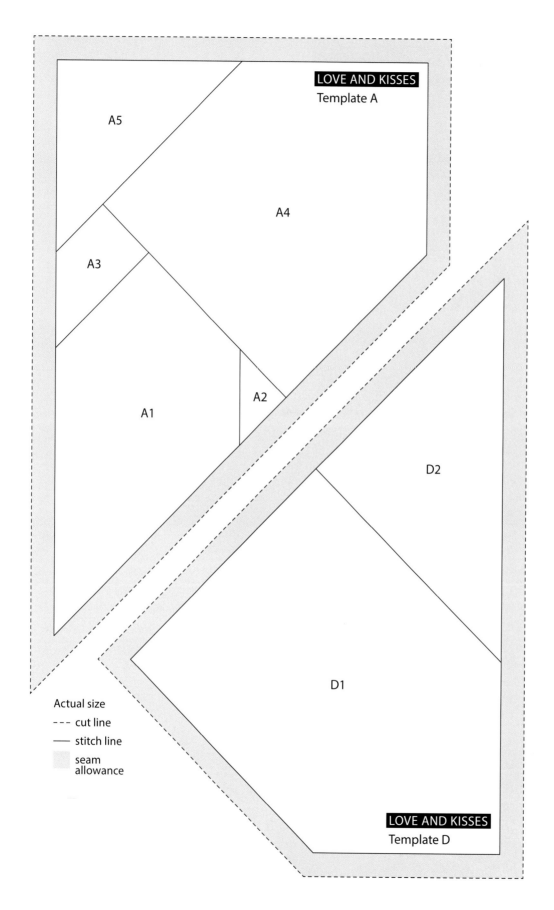

LOVE AND KISSES

Template A

A5

A4

A3

A1

A2

D2

D1

LOVE AND KISSES

Template D

Actual size

- - - cut line

——— stitch line

seam
allowance

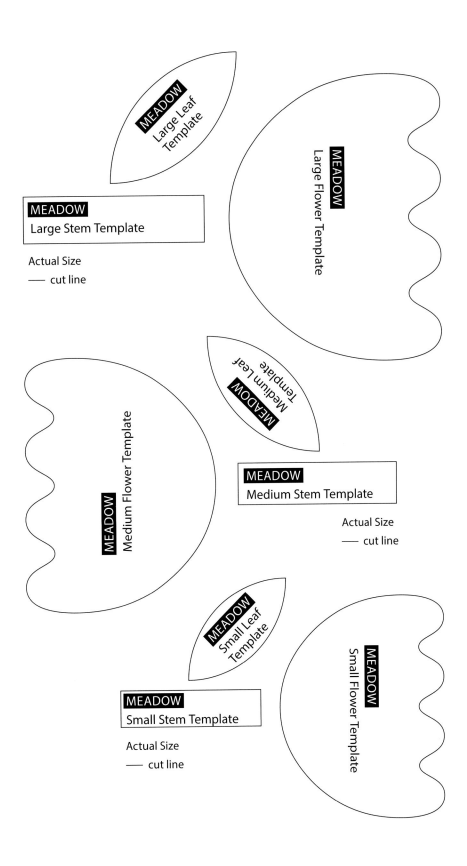

MEADOW
Large Leaf Template

MEADOW
Large Flower Template

MEADOW
Large Stem Template

Actual Size
—— cut line

MEADOW
Medium Flower Template

MEADOW
Medium Leaf Template

MEADOW
Medium Stem Template

Actual Size
—— cut line

MEADOW
Small Leaf Template

MEADOW
Small Stem Template

MEADOW
Small Flower Template

Actual Size
—— cut line

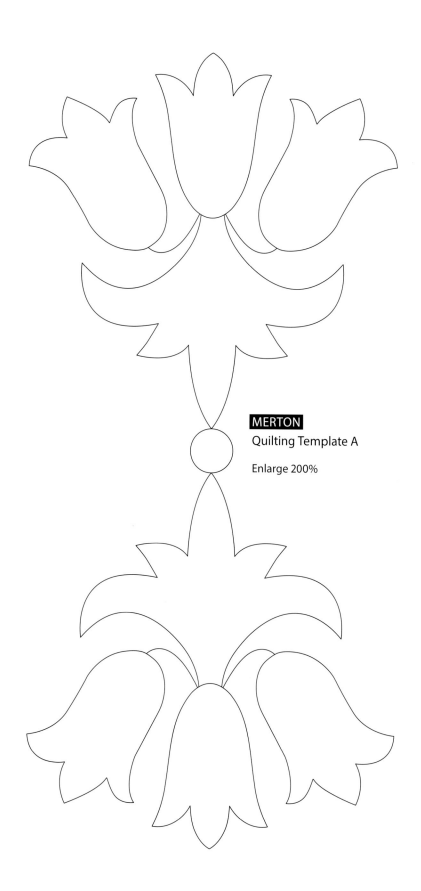

MERTON

Quilting Template A

Enlarge 200%

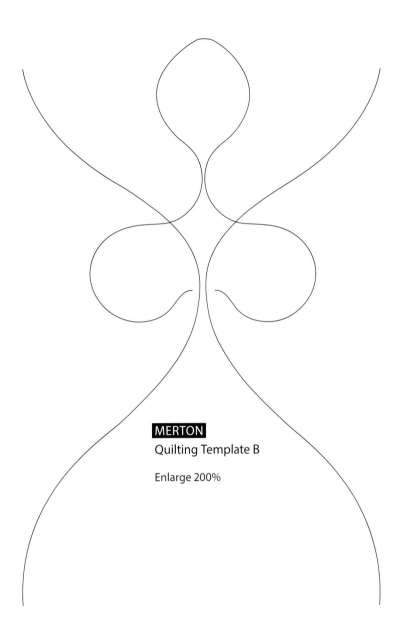

MERTON

Quilting Template B

Enlarge 200%

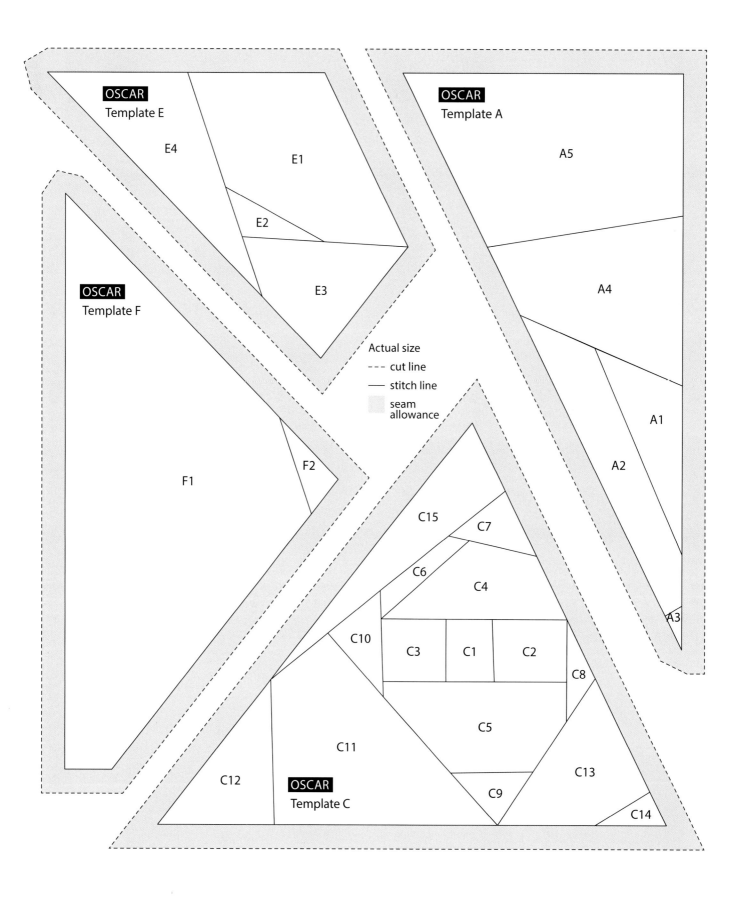

OSCAR
Template E

E4

E1

E2

E3

OSCAR
Template A

A5

A4

A1

A2

A3

OSCAR
Template F

F1

F2

Actual size
- - - cut line
——— stitch line
seam allowance

C15

C7

C6

C4

C10

C3   C1   C2

C8

C5

C11

C13

OSCAR
Template C

C12

C9

C14

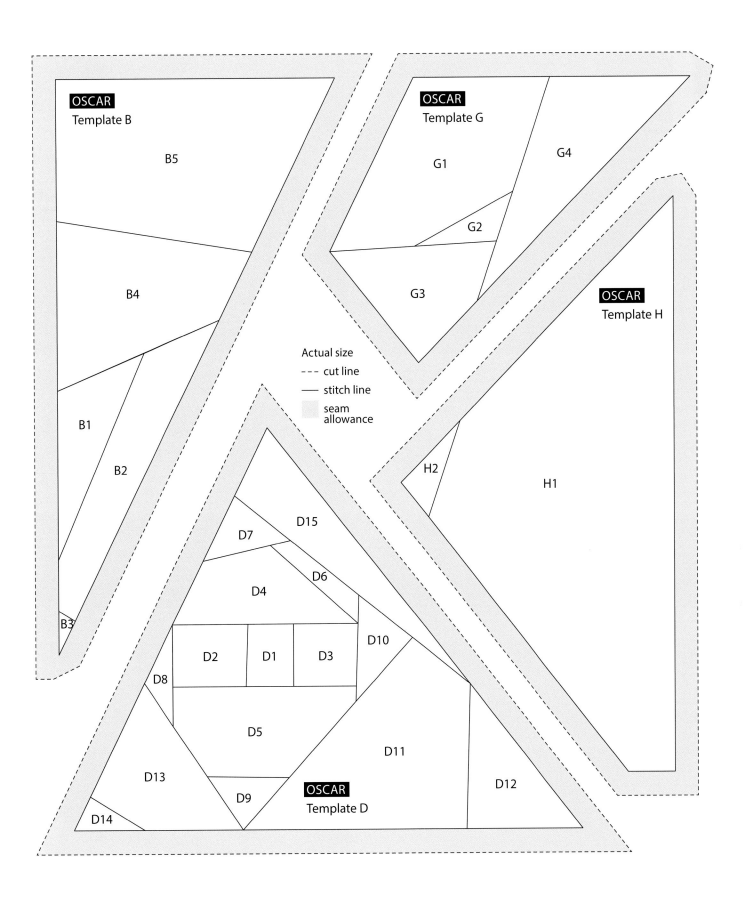

OSCAR
Template B

B5

B4

B1

B2

B3

OSCAR
Template G

G1

G4

G2

G3

OSCAR
Template H

H2

H1

Actual size
- - - cut line
—— stitch line
█ seam
allowance

D15

D7

D6

D4

D10

D2 D1 D3

D8

D5

D11

D13

D9

OSCAR
Template D

D12

D14

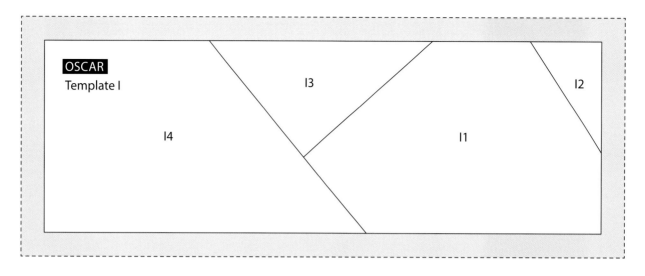

OSCAR
Template I

I3

I2

I4

I1

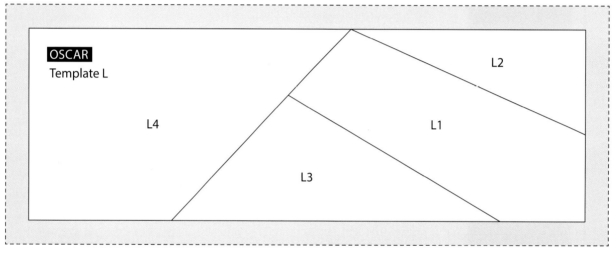

OSCAR
Template L

L2

L4

L1

L3

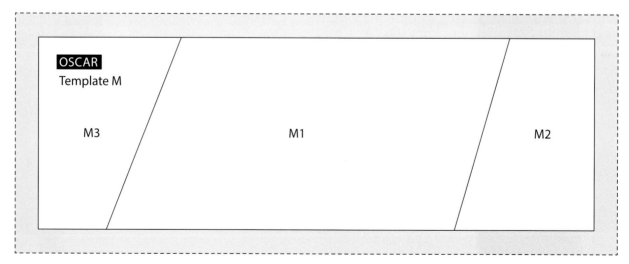

OSCAR
Template M

M3

M1

M2

Actual size

- - - cut line

—— stitch line

seam allowance

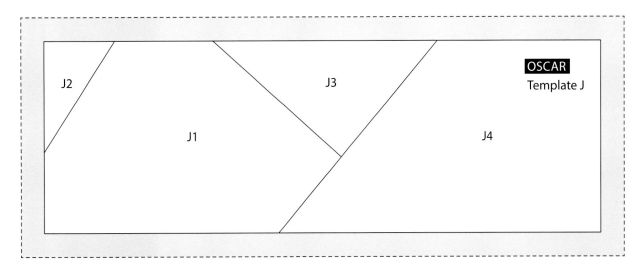

OSCAR
Template J

J2   J3   J1   J4

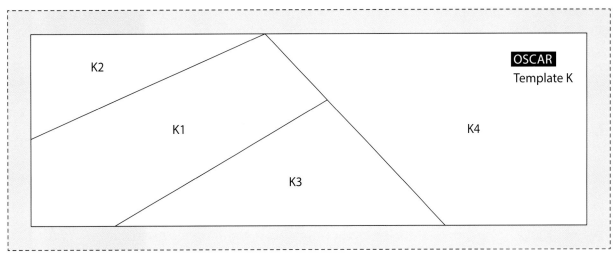

OSCAR
Template K

K2   K1   K3   K4

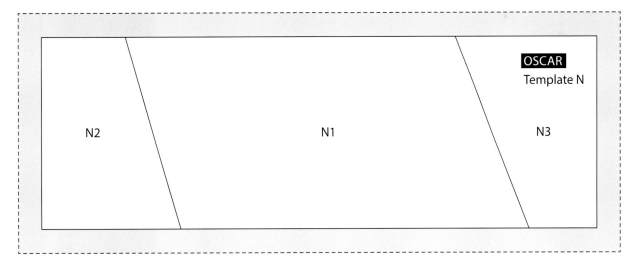

OSCAR
Template N

N2   N1   N3

Actual size

--- cut line

—— stitch line

seam allowance

RESOURCES

Here are some useful websites for finding my favourite sewing supplies.

AURIFIL
aurifil.com
Thread

BEYOND MEASURE
shopbeyondmeasure.co.uk
Haberdashery

DAYLIGHT COMPANY
daylightcompany.com
Daylight lamps and
lightboxes

ERNEST WRIGHT
ernestwright.co.uk
Scissors

FOXGLOVE AND FIELD
foxgloveandfield.co.uk
Pattern weights

IRIS HANTWERK
irishantwerk.se
Table brush set

JANOME
janome.co.uk
Sewing machines

JENNI SMITH
jenni-smith.co.uk
Patterns and quilt templates

JUST ONE QUILT
justonequilt.com
Online quilt courses with
Jenni Smith

LIBERTY FABRICS
Shop: libertylondon.com
Wholesale: libertyfabric.com
@libertyfabrics
#libertycraftclub

OAKSHOTT
oakshottfabrics.com
Shot cottons

OLFA
olfa.com
Cutting mats, rotary
cutters and rulers

PROJECT WOOL
projectwool.com
Wool pressing mats

ROBERT KAUFMAN
robertkaufman.com
Kona quilting cottons
and Essex linen

WARM COMPANY
warmcompany.com
Batting

ABOUT THE AUTHOR

JENNI SMITH is a teacher, quilter and dressmaking pattern designer with a busy studio in Yorkshire. Her dream is to inspire everyone to make Just One Quilt in their lifetime and she encourages this through online workshops, engaging short films and lectures. Jenni has loved Liberty Fabrics since visiting their mill shop in Lancashire as a child and is excited to have had their support in the creation of her debut book.

ACKNOWLEDGEMENTS

The best takeaway I have from this project is the people who helped to make it happen and I love that the quilts are bound with happy memories of late night sewing, endless rounds of Yorkshire tea and way too many cakes.

Kay Walsh you are incredible. Many times I burst into the studio with handfuls of uncategorized notebooks brimming with ideas, just as I did with this book, and every time you helped to make those dreams a reality. Your dedication and patience deserves a medal or two and I promise to be tidier now that our stitching marathon is complete!

Paul, thank you for living amongst my creative chaos for the past 20 years and for giving me time to nourish my hobby slowly and without pressure so that I could gain confidence and start my own business.

Harry, Edie and Ellis: the desire to make you all quilts to snuggle under was what got me into all of this so you deserve a big thank you. You also did a brilliant job of removing papers from the foundation pieced blocks so you have all had a hand in this book.

Bradley you are my guardian angel in the quilting world and are always a trusted friend who listens and makes me smile. Please move back to Yorkshire soon.

My sewing ladies who came to my rescue and helped to finish several of the quilts — well I dread what might have happened if you weren't in town! Thank you especially to Anne, Caroline, Deborah, Dorothy, Jeanette, Julia, Nim, Margaret and Suzanne.

Thank you Trudi Wood and Debs McGuire for adding a whole new creative element to the book with your long-arming skills.

Jenny and Karen our day of cracking curves together was a special one, and came at just the right time to power me through the final makes.

Mum, Pat, Laura, Caroline, Sarah and Nicky thanks for entertaining the kids whilst I stitched away and for always asking how I am getting on.

Team Liberty I am grateful for your belief that we could make a beautiful book together and your creative input has been invaluable. Thank-you Adam, Anna, Elle, Eleonora, Jalil, Mary-Ann and Pauline.

Susanne — I knew from our first trans-Atlantic telephone call that you were the best person to make this book with. Thank you for challenging me and looking after me in equal measure. Thank you also to the rest of the Lucky Spool Team — Rae Ann, Kari and Yvonne.

Nissa and Kristy @pageandpixel — I am so pleased that you travelled from California to the UK to style and photograph the quilts in the book. It was a privilege to watch you in action.

Thank you Deborah and the Janome team, Michael and Gill at Oakshott and Andrew at Littondale.

Aurifil — not only do we have the best times together, your thread is a dream. Special thanks to Alex and Erin.

Finally, thank you everybody who has come to my quilting classes over the years. Teaching has given me the confidence to follow my dream and to write this book. All of our shared experience is of enormous value to me, and I couldn't have done it without you.

"I was determined not to follow existing fashion but to create new ones."

— ARTHUR LASENBY LIBERTY

I hope this book inspires you to put your own personal spin on a quilt project and create something bold and unique for the future.

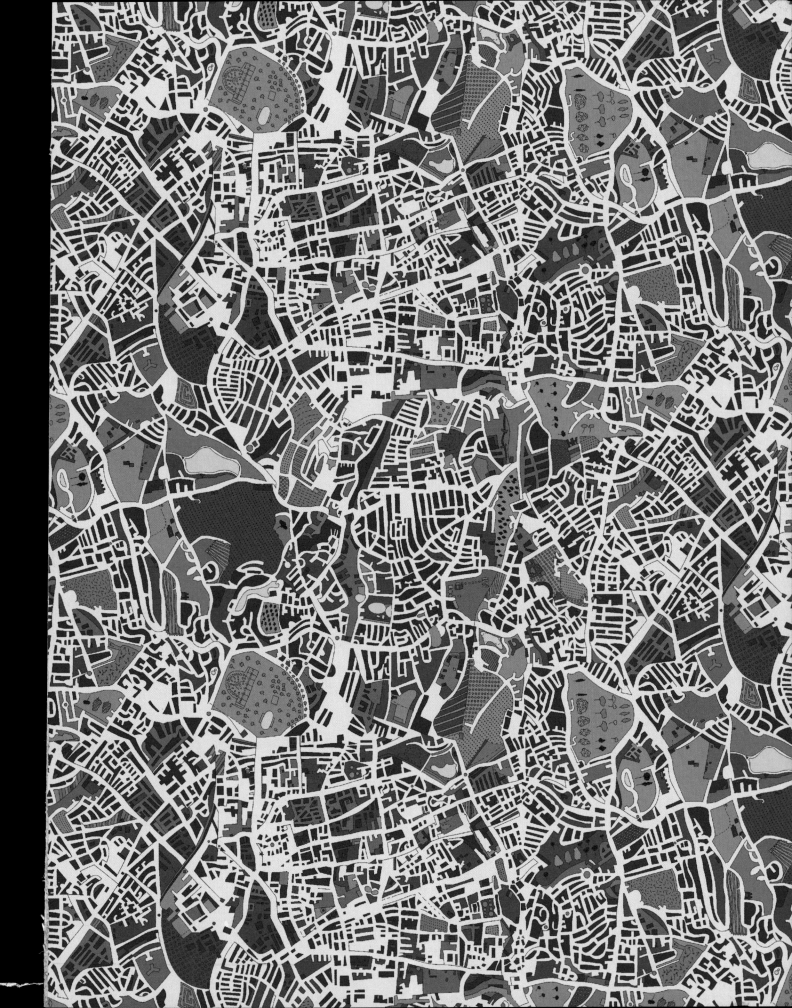